I0410537

How to become an influent person.

Book content:

2

Prologue

Personal influence helps us very much in many situations to accomplish personal objectives and many successes big or small.

Personal influence can be formed, developed and maintained.

Personal influence is a big or small richness, according to how much we succeeded to form and develop it.

In life and for as long as we live it is necessary to have as a personal objective to develop personal influence.

Personal influence is also a part of the power that everybody has or as we might say, it creates personal power.

Increasing the personal influence, we can increase the personal power.

Personal power helps us in life to accomplish much faster all personal objectives and more successes.

Personal influence can contribute very much to accomplish a more beautiful and pleasant life.

AGC thoughts and the ideas from this book and the others that follow, help us very much to increase personal influence.

The money invested in this book of mine and the others that follow it is worth it, and it is almost nothing comparing to the positive effects that this book can have in your life, by applying the ideas to your life.

This volumes must be bought and used day by day, in order to development your personality and to the accomplish of all that you want.

These books contain lots of positive, optimist, creative, dynamic ideas, that push you to action, to thinking, things that are necessary your daily life and to accomplish your personal objectives.

Reading and analyzing the ideas in this book and applying them, we'll find solutions and ideas that will help us find:

I. To discover:

    1. qualities

    2. defects

    3. capabilities

    4. qualifications

5. some opportunities to succeed in life

6. feelings

7. what we do to be loved

8. how to love

9. how to realize and maintain a true mutual love

10. how to realize and maintain a happy marriage

11. mistakes, errors, wrong ideas

12. etc.

II. To prevent some:

1. divorces

2. mistakes

3. suspect

4. grief's

5. conflicts

6. accidents

7. failures

8. bankruptcy

9. etc.

III. To become more:
1. happy
2. loved
3. honored,
4. appreciated,
5. wanted,
6. optimistic,
7. good,
8. unselfish,
9. emotional,
10. altruists
11. stronger
12. efficient
13. organized
14. planners
15. active
16. honest
17. human
18. popular
19. famous
20. flexible
21. adaptable

22. understanding

23. prompt

24. etc.

IV. To get out of a state of:

1. despair

2. pessimism

3. passiveness

4. inactivity

5. inefficiency

6. inflexibility

7. crisis

8. inadaptability

9. etc.

V. To participate more actively to:

1. social life

2. political life

3. nonprofit organizations activities

4. etc

VI. To participate more actively and efficiently in achieving true love and a happy marriage

VII.　To find more likely situations conducive to achieving and maintaining a happy marriage life

VIII.　To change our life for the better and to make it more beautiful

IX.　To multiply and increase the chances to find your life partner

X.　To raise and educate our children better so we can take better care of them

XI.　Find more and bigger chances to meet favorable situations to accomplish and maintain a happy marriage for life.

XII.　Change our life in good and make it better.

XIII.　To multiply and increase the chances to find your life partner

XIV.　To raise and educate our children better so we can take better care of them

I write and gather these thoughts, ideas in books, internet and other publications because these are useful to us every day and it is necessary to apply them to accomplish what we want, a better and beautiful life and prosperous.

These thoughts reflect a small part of what is good in reality and human relationships.

I wait to hear from you good news, good deeds that you have done influenced from what you have read from these books to make your life more beautiful, prosperous, happier and to be a positive example for others.

Each of us can become positive examples for others around us, participating to the creation of a better, prosperous and happier human society.

I'd be happy if one or more ideas read from these books helped you in a way or another and made you happier and prosperous.

I'm waiting to hear from you, your ideas and opinions, your joys and grieves and your suggestions for new book subjects and I also appeal to your participation of promoting on the internet and mass media of the ideas and the books I've written.

I invite you to e-mail me at my email address: agcornel@gmail.com.

Dear readers I wish you all health, happiness and achievement of all your wishes.

Best regards and respect,

Gheorghe Cornel Ardelean

981 Principal Street
Macea, Arad county
Zip Code 371210
Romania
Tel # (40)-0788-725-204
(40)-0788-725-913

Abilities

1. Our abilities can be form, develop, maintain and use also through the contribution of the formation, development, maintenance and usage of the ability to relax.

2. In order to pursue and transform our personal goals into reality we need to form and develop the necessary abilities for efficient global co operations.

3. The necessary abilities, including those necessary to achieve our personal goals, can be formed, developed, maintained and used also through the contribution of the formation, development, maintenance and usage have the ability to organize efficiently.

4. Abilities can be formed, developed, maintained and used also through the contribution of the formation, development, maintenance and usage of cooperative behaviors.

5. Abilities can be formed, developed, maintained and used also through the contribution of the formation, development, maintenance and usage of the ability of rapid perception.

6. The necessary abilities to achieve our goals can be formed also through the ability to face stress.

7. Abilities can be developed also through using efficient and behaviors.

8. Abilities can be developed also through using efficient behaviors.

9. Abilities can be formed through prevision.

10. Abilities can be formed through positive behaviors.

11. The abilities that we need including those to achieve personal goals can be formed, developed, maintained and used through the contribution of the formation, development, maintenance and usage of the ability to find solutions to problems we want to solve.

12. Abilities can be formed, developed, maintained and used also through the contribution of the formation, development, maintenance and usage of a constructive life conception.

13. Abilities can be formed, developed, maintained and used also through the contribution of the formation, development,

maintenance and usage of the ability to face responsibilities.

14. By listening very carefully to what people who have had successes say and by taking useful ideas from them we can form, develop, maintain and use the abilities to create cooperation in a team.

15. Abilities can be formed with the contribution of logical behaviors.

16. Our abilities can be developed by using the capacity to influence people.

17. Emancipation from restrictions can be made through the formation, development and support of efficient abilities.

18. The necessary abilities to achieve personal goals can be formed, developed, maintained and used also through the contribution of the formation, development, maintenance and usage of an orderly behavior.

19. Abilities can be formed, developed, maintained and used also through the contribution of forming, development and usage of confident behaviors.

20. AGC mediations help us discover abilities.

Accomplishments

21. We can contribute to the achievement of our greatest accomplishments also through the contribution of the formation, development, maintenance and usage of inventive behavior.

22. We can contribute to the achievement of our greatest accomplishments also through the contribution of the formation, development, maintenance and usage of continuous self-motivating behavior.

23. We can contribute to the achievement of our greatest accomplishments also through the contribution of the formation, development, maintenance and usage of expansive behavior.

24. We can contribute to the achievement of our greatest accomplishments also through the contribution of the formation, development, maintenance and usage of sociable behavior.

25. We can contribute to the achievement of our greatest accomplishments also through the contribution of the formation, development,

maintenance and usage of unpretentious behavior.

26.   We can contribute to the achievement of our greatest accomplishments also through the contribution of the formation, development, maintenance and usage of profound behavior.

27.   We can contribute to the achievement of our greatest accomplishments also through the contribution of the formation, development, maintenance and usage of being an efficient negotiator behavior.

28.   We can contribute to the achievement of our greatest accomplishments also through the contribution of the formation, development, maintenance and usage of peaceful behavior.

29.   We can contribute to the achievement of our greatest accomplishments also through the contribution of the formation, development, maintenance and usage of a behavior of being in love with life.

30.   We can contribute to the achievement of our greatest accomplishments also through the contribution of the formation, development,

maintenance and usage of animated behavior.

31. We can contribute to the achievement of our greatest accomplishments also through the contribution of the formation, development, maintenance and usage of consequent behavior.

32. We can contribute to the achievement of our greatest accomplishments also through the contribution of the formation, development, maintenance and usage of diligent behavior.

33. We can contribute to the achievement of our greatest accomplishments also through the contribution of the formation, development, maintenance and usage of receptive to new behavior.

34. We can contribute to the achievement of our greatest accomplishments also through the contribution of the formation, development, maintenance and usage of sportive behavior. We can contribute to the achievement of our greatest accomplishments also through the contribution of the formation, development, maintenance and usage of firm behavior.

35. We can contribute to the achievement of our greatest accomplishments also through the contribution of the formation, development, maintenance and usage of initiating behavior.

36. We can contribute to the achievement of our greatest accomplishments also through the contribution of the formation, development, maintenance and usage of conscientious behavior.

Adaptability

37. In order to transform positive objectives into reality it is necessary to form, develop, maintain and use the sense of adaptability.

38. The limits we have set can be overcome by the formation, development, maintenance and usage of the sense of adaptability.

39. In order to change our life it is necessary to form, develop, maintain and use the sense of adaptability.

40. Our transformation for the better can be achieved also through the contribution of the

formation, development, maintenance and usage of adaptability to each situation.

41. People who have not succeeded in obtaining a happy marriage must develop their sense of adaptability.

42. Those who have high objectives in life mostly have the sense of adaptability.

Actions

43. Openness towards new efficient actions helps us achieve much good luck.

44. Effective daily actions that are completed with passion help us achieve more successes.

45. Our everyday effective actions help us achieve more efficient co operations.

46. Effective daily actions that are completed with passion help us achieve more favorable chances.

47. Our everyday effective actions help us achieve more successes.

48. Imitating efficient actions helps us achieve more performances.

49. Our everyday effective actions help us achieve more pleasant surprises.

50. Imitating efficient actions helps us achieve much good luck.

51. Openness towards new efficient actions helps us achieve more performances.

52. Our everyday effective actions help us achieve more personal goals.

53. Our everyday effective actions help us achieve more favorable situations.

54. Openness towards new efficient actions helps us achieve more favorable chances.

55. Our everyday effective actions help us achieve more performances.

56. Imitating efficient actions helps us achieve more favorable chances.

57. Openness towards new efficient actions helps us achieve more true friendships.

58. Imitating efficient actions helps us achieve more successes.

59. The actions of prevention of human errors must be promoted.

60. The actions of prevention of human errors must be supported.

61. The actions of prevention of human errors must be learned.

62. We can achieve a happy life only through positive effective actions.

63. Effective co operations and developments are due to very positive effective actions.

64. It is necessary for children to learn continuously, day by day, only positive effective actions.

65. Positive effective actions are those that carry out personal objectives.

66. Positive effective actions maintain a happy marriage.

67. Success is obtained only with positive effective actions.

Activities

68.   Skill must be developed continuously in the activities we achieve.

69.   In order to pursue and transform our personal goals into reality we need to form, develop, maintain and use the ability to be cooperative in the activities that we have.

70.   Those who have high objectives in life are mostly people who are used to carry out the activities they have started.

71.   Those who have high objectives in life are cooperative in activities.

72.   In order to trace and transform our personal goals into reality it is necessary to form, develop, maintain and use the ability to be cooperative in the activities we have.

73.   Obstacles that stop us from achieving our personal goals can be overcome also through the contribution of the formation, development, maintenance and usage of the ability to be cooperative in activities.

74.   A cooperative man in activities achieves more efficient co operations.

75. People who are used to carry out the activities they have started have the ability to achieve a happy marriage.

76. People who are used to carry out the activities they have started more easily maintain true friendships.

77. People who are used to carry out the activities they have started are reliable people.

78. People who are used to carry out the activities they have started must be appreciated, promoted, supported and rewarded.

79. People who are used to carry out the activities they have started contribute a lot in achieving the greater good.

80. People who are used to carrying out the activities they have started have the possibility to become happy.

81. People who are used to carry out the activities they have started have the possibility to become happy.

82. People who are used to carrying out the activities they had started have a high capacity to prevent many failures.

83. People who are used to carrying out the activities they had started have greater chances to achieve more and greater successes.

84. People who are used to carrying out the activities they had started are the engines of progress in all fields of activity.

85. People who are used to carrying out the activities they had started have a high potential to achieve their desired future.

86. Working in teams of people with similar values is an engine of progress in common activities.

87. The man who is cooperative in activities has greater chances to prevent more failures.

88. In all countries the number and quality of non-profit organizations activities must increase greatly and continuously as they can contribute greatly to the development of

many problems in each country and in the world.

Adaptation

89. Our ability of optimal adaptation helps us achieve more efficient co operations.

90. The ability of optimal adaptation very much increases our possibility to achieve more true friendships.

91. The ability of optimal adaptation increases our possibilities maintain a happy marriage.

92. The desire to make others happy can be accomplished through the contribution of the formation, development, maintenance and usage of the sense of adaptation.

93. Adaptation helps us achieve more successes.

94. Adaptation helps us maintain happiness.

95. Adaptation must be a model.

96. Adaptation helps us become more loving.

97. Adaptation helps us achieve a happy marriage.

98. Adaptation helps us become tolerant.

99. Adaptation helps us maintain the way of being loving.

100. Adaptation helps us maintain the way of being understanding.

101. Adaptation helps us become more humane.

102. Adaptation must be appreciated.

103. Adaptation helps us achieve more true friendships.

104. Adaptation helps us maintain efficiency.

Ambitious

105. By having ambitious friends we sometimes become more ambitious.

106. People who have had successes are mostly very ambitious.

107. The majority of ambitious people succeed in achieving a more beautiful life.

108. Ambitious people have a greater potential to become even more efficient.

109. Ambitious men have a greater potential to achieve their personal goals.

110. Ambitious people have much more chances to meet more favorable situations.

111. An ambitious man has great chances of achieving the desired future.

112. Ambitious people must be appreciated, promoted, supported and rewarded.

113. An ambitious man more easily makes social relations.

Analytic

114. In order to rise up once again for the first time for the who knows what time it is necessary to also form, develop, maintain and use analytic behavior.

115. Our happiness depends a lot also on the formation, development, maintenance and usage of analytic behavior.

116. Our own happiness can be achieved and maintained also through the contribution of the formation, development, maintenance and usage of analytic behavior.

117. Acting efficiently helps us become analytical.

118. The radical transformation for the better of our life can be achieved also through the formation, development, maintenance and usage of analytic behavior.

119. In order to escape poverty it is necessary to also form, develop, maintain and use an analytical thinking behavior.

120. In order to prevent not achieving our personal goals, it is necessary to also form, develop, maintain and use our analytic behavior.

121. Some mistakes can be prevented also through the contribution of the formation, development, maintenance and usage of analytic behavior.

122. In order to prevent failures it is necessary to also form, develop, maintain and use analytical behavior.

123. Continuous self-control helps us become analytic.

124. Cherishing oneself helps us become analytic.

125. Hope helps us become analytic.

126. The analytic spirit has a great contribution to achieving our success in life.

127. The analytics spirit increases our power.

128. Problems cannot be solved by the ideas that created them but through the contribution of the formation, development, maintenance and usage of analytic spirit.

129. In order to follow and transform our personal goals into reality, it is necessary to also form, develop, maintain and use our analytic behavior.

130. Confidence in ourselves helps us become analytic.

131. Problems cannot be solved by the ideas that created them but also through the contribution of the formation, development, maintenance and usage of analytic behavior.

132. Stress can be prevented also through the formation, development, maintenance and usage of analytic behavior.

133. Creativity helps us become analytic.

134. Aspiring towards a more meaningful life can also be achieved through the formation, development, maintenance and usage of analytic behavior.

135. Continuous self-motivation helps us become analytical.

136. In order to escape poverty it is necessary to also form, develop, maintain and use analytic behavior.

137. Obtaining more and greater successes can be achieved also through the contribution of the formation, development, maintenance, usage of an analytic behavior.

138. Hopes can be created also through the contribution of the formation, development, maintenance and usage of analytic behavior.

139. The obstacles that prevent us from achieving our personal goals can be surpassed also through the contribution of the formation, development, maintenance and usage of analytic behavior.

140. Will helps us become analytic.

141. Rather than lamenting that we do not have successes it is more useful to also form, develop, maintain and use analytic behavior.

142. Continuous self-motivation helps us become analytic.

143. The limits of achievement imposed by ourselves in our mind at a given moment can be overcome or eliminated also through the contribution of the formation, development, maintenance and usage of analytic behavior.

144. Acting efficiently helps us become analytic.

145. Obtaining more and greater successes can be achieved also through the contribution of the formation, development, maintenance, usage of analytical thinking.

146. Our future can be projected and achieved also through the contribution of the formation, development, maintenance and usage of analytic behavior.

147. Wisdom helps us become analytic.

148. Self-imposed discipline helps us become analytic.

149. Continuous self perfection helps us become analytic.

150. Positive experience can be achieved also through the contribution of the formation, development, maintenance and usage of analytic behavior.

151. Continuously making ourselves efficient helps us become analytic.

152. Pessimism can be removed and replaced with optimism also through the contribution of the formation, development, maintenance and usage of analytic behavior.

153. Our resistance to changing for the better can be overcome also through the contribution of the formation, development, maintenance and usage of analytic behavior.

Aspirations

154. Aspirations towards a more meaningful life can be achieved also through the contribution of the formation, development, maintenance and usage of the ability to cope with stressing situations.

155. Aspirations toward a more meaningful life can be achieved also through the contribution of the formation, development, maintenance and usage of the ability to create, develop and maintain hopes.

Attitudes

156. A great capacity of using attitudes must be encouraged.

157. A great capacity of using attitudes helps us become loved.

158. A great capacity of using attitudes helps us maintain our tolerance.

159. A great capacity of using attitudes helps us become efficient.

160. A great capacity of using attitudes helps us maintain our wisdom.

161. A great capacity of using attitudes helps us maintain our happiness.

162. A great capacity of using attitudes helps us maintain our way of being understanding.

163. A great capacity of using attitudes helps us maintain our enthusiasm.

164. A great capacity of using attitudes helps us become optimistic.

165. A great capacity of using attitudes helps us become tolerant.

166. A great capacity of using attitudes must be maintained.

167. A great capacity of using attitudes must be a model.

168. A great capacity of using attitudes helps us become more loving.

169. A great capacity of using attitudes helps us become more enthusiastic.

170. Young people from all of the world's states should not be negligent, careless, passive, inactive, non-participative in taking decisions that concern them, their present and future, but to take part in decision-making in local councils, central parliaments, governments and other state and non-state institutions, and use all their capacities, abilities, skills, attitudes, knowledge, energy, commitment and desire to assert and achieve great

deeds, to create a more humane, more righteous, more happy, with less trouble world.

171. Where necessary, it is good to change attitudes and behavior because only so we can achieve happiness.

172. It is always needed to develop capacities, skills, qualities and attitudes, but we need the development of our personality, it is necessary to have this as a personal objective.

173. The creative attitudes that we do not have we must form to help us become more creative.

174. We can create a beautiful life for ourselves if we have creative attitudes.

Become

175. The desire to become even more effective helps us achieve more personal goals.

176. The desire to become even more effective helps us achieve more favorable situations.

177. The desire to become even more effective helps us achieve more true friendships.

178. The desire to become even more performing helps us achieve more efficient co operations.

179. The desire to become even more performing helps us achieve more performances.

180. The desire to become even more effective helps us achieve more pleasant surprises.

181. The desire to become even more effective helps us achieve more records.

182. The desire to become even more performing helps us achieve more pleasant surprises.

183. The desire to become even more performing helps us achieve much good luck.

184. The desire to become even more performing helps us achieve more favorable situations.

185. The desire to become even more effective helps us achieve more favorable chances.

186. The desire to become even more effective helps us achieve more performances.

187. The desire to become even more performing helps us achieve more successes.

188. The desire to become even more performing helps us achieve more true friendships.

189. The desire to become even more effective helps us achieve more successes.

190. Self-imposed discipline helps us become good listeners.

191. Will helps us become respectful.

192. A great capacity of more efficiently using time helps us become productive.

193. Acting efficiently helps us become mannered.

Behavior

194. Those who have a good behavior help us achieve more true friendships.

195. Preventing negative behaviors helps us achieve more personal goals.

196. Those who have a good behavior help us achieve more personal goals.

197. Preventing negative behaviors helps us achieve more performances.

198. Those who have a good behavior help us achieve much good luck.

199. Those who have a good behavior help us achieve more records.

200. Preventing negative behaviors helps us achieve more favorable situations.

201. Preventing negative behaviors helps us achieve more efficient co operations.

202. Those who have a good behavior help us achieve more efficient co operations.

203. Preventing negative behaviors helps us achieve more pleasant surprises.

204. Those who have a good behavior help us achieve more favorable chances.

205. Those who have a good behavior help us achieve more pleasant surprises.

206. Preventing negative behaviors helps us achieve much good luck.

207. Those who have a good behavior help us achieve more favorable situations.

208. Preventing negative behaviors helps us achieve more favorable chances.

209. Preventing negative behaviors helps us achieve more successes.

210. Those who have a good behavior help us achieve more performances.

211. Preventing negative behaviors helps us achieve more true friendships.

212. Preventing negative behaviors helps us achieve more records.

213. Release from our self-imposed restrictions can be made also through the contribution of the formation, development, maintenance and usage of positive behavior.

214. The solutions to the problems we have or that we want to solve can be found also through the contribution of the formation, development, maintenance and usage of selfless behavior.

215. Pessimism can be removed and replaced with optimism also through the contribution of the formation, development, maintenance and usage of continuous self-controlling behavior.

216. Aspiring towards a more meaningful life can also be achieved through the formation,

development, maintenance and usage of strong behavior.

217. Stress can be prevented also through the formation, development, maintenance and usage of diplomatic behavior.

218. The necessary qualities in achieving personal goals can be formed, developed, maintained and used also through the contribution of the formation, development, maintenance and usage of self-controlled behavior.

Bold

219. We can overcome the difficulties that we must overcome also through the help of the formation, development, maintenance and usage of bold behavior.

220. Positive experience can be achieved also through the contribution of the formation, development, maintenance and usage of bold behavior.

221. In achieving our successes a contribution is also brought by the formation, development, maintenance and usage of bold behavior.

222. Continuous self-control helps us become bold.

223. Communication helps us become bold.

224. Creativity helps us become bold.

225. Cherishing oneself helps us become bold.

226. The necessary qualities in achieving personal goals can be formed, developed, maintained and used also through the contribution of the formation, development, maintenance and usage of bold behavior.

227. Release from our self-imposed restrictions can be made also through the contribution of the formation, development, maintenance and usage of bold behavior.

228. We can form, develop and maintain the state of being ourselves also through the contribution of the formation, development, maintenance and usage of a bold behavior.

229. Brutality harm us very much.

Believe

230. Positive imagination can help us achieve more therefore we can believe that we are able to achieve more.

231. People who have had successes in life have mostly believed in their success.

232. People who have had successes in life have mostly believed in people.

233. When we believe in certain values we feel happy.

234. Those who believe that others are to blame for their mistakes are illogical in that rationality.

235. People who help others, most of the times help them because they believe it is good and necessary and not obligatory.

236. Fatigue can be prevented through the proper nutrition of the person concerned, through education, positive behavior, balanced life, intellectual exercises, perseverance, willpower, exercise, a value system that we believe in and that we respect, business dynamism, social relations, friends, mature

love, a happy marriage, adequate rest when necessary, proper sleep, entertainment, etc..

237. People's creative thinking will solve many global problems today in a period of time much smaller than almost all the people today believe they would.

238. Creative thinking can find solutions to many problems that we believe to be impossible to resolve.

239. The facts that are incredible to achieve and that have been achieved show us that many problems that many people still have at the moment can be certainly solved if they believe that they can resolve them if they act with dedication to their resolution.

240. Most people who performe incredible deeds had achieved that incredible objective that they believed in and to which they have dedicated themselved until they have achieved it.

241. People who live from hand to mouth do not have realistic objectives on a long term in which to believe and to whom to dedicate themselves to achieve.

242. Those who do not have realistic objectives to believe in and act with dedication to achieve them, they do not believe in the future.

243. When we have realistic goals that we believe in and act with dedication to achieve them, some of us feel happy.

244. When we have realistic goals that we believe in and act with dedication to achieve them, we are confident in our future.

Brave

245. A great capacity of being brave helps us maintain our productivity.

246. A great capacity of being brave helps us become more enthusiastic.

247. A great capacity of being brave helps us become happy.

248. Pessimism can be removed and replaced with optimism also through the contribution of the formation, development, maintenance and usage of brave behavior.

249. A great capacity of being brave helps us become more efficient.

250. Problems cannot be solved by the ideas that created them but also through the contribution of the formation, development, maintenance and usage of brave behavior.

251. A great capacity of being brave must be appreciated.

252. A great capacity of being brave helps us become efficient.

253. A great capacity of being brave helps us become wise.

254. We can overcome the difficulties that we must overcome also through the help of the formation, development, maintenance and usage of brave behavior.

255. Our future can be projected and achieved also through the contribution of the formation, development, maintenance and usage of brave behavior.

256. A great capacity of being brave helps us maintain our way of being loved.

257. Our happiness depends a lot also on the formation, development, maintenance and usage of brave behavior.

258. A great capacity of being brave helps us maintain our wisdom.

259. A great capacity of being brave must be maintained.

260. A great capacity of being brave helps us become cautious.

261. Hopes can be created also through the contribution of the formation, development, maintenance and usage of brave behavior.

Behave

262. In life, we must not behave like x or y says, but according to the way we think it is best, positive, correct, legal and human.

263. When the husband behaves badly with his wife and hates her, he alienates her from him.

264. Patience and the art of behaving patient is part of our wisdom. It is necessary to

continuously develop the capacity to endure and the art to behave with patience.

265. If some men would behave properly with women, there would be much less divorces and unhappy marriages in the world.

Beliefs

266. The strength of going against everybody's beliefs helps us achieve much good luck.

267. The strength of going against everybody's beliefs helps us achieve more successes.

268. The will of going against everyone else's beliefs helps us achieve more pleasant surprises.

269. The will of going against everyone else's beliefs helps us achieve more favorable situations.

270. The strength of going against everybody's beliefs helps us achieve more records.

271. Some successes are the effects of beliefs.

272. The strength of going against everybody's beliefs helps us achieve more true friendships.

273. Many problems can be avoided by the beliefs that we have.

Calm

274. Pessimism can be removed and replaced with optimism also through the contribution of the formation, development, maintenance and usage of calm behavior.

275. Our own happiness can be achieved and maintained also through the contribution of the formation, development, maintenance and usage of calm behavior.

276. Positive experience can be achieved also through the contribution of the formation, development, maintenance and usage of calm behavior.

277. The force of our ideas can be augmented also through the contribution of the formation, development, maintenance and usage of calm behavior.

278. In order to prevent not achieving our personal goals, it is necessary to also form, develop, maintain and use our calm behavior.

279. Aspiring towards a more meaningful life can also be achieved through the formation, development, maintenance and usage of calm behavior.

280. Our resistance to changing for the better can be overcome also through the contribution of the formation, development, maintenance and usage of calm behavior.

281. We can prevent the falling apart of a happy marriage also through the contribution of the formation, development, maintenance and usage of calm behavior.

282. Hopes can be created also through the contribution of the formation, development, maintenance and usage of calm behavior.

283. We can overcome the difficulties that we must overcome also through the help of the formation, development, maintenance and usage of calm behavior.

284. We can become stronger and we can not allow ourselves to be influenced by the world also through the contribution of the formation, development, maintenance and usage of calm behavior.

285. In achieving our successes a contribution is also brought by the formation, development, maintenance and usage of calm behavior.

286. We can contribute to the achievement of our greatest accomplishments also through the contribution of the formation, development, maintenance and usage of calm behavior.

Capacities

287. Our necessary capacities including those necessary to the achievement of personal objectives can be formed, developed, maintained and used through the contribution of the formation, development, maintenance and usage of the ability to efficiently organize.

288. Those who control circumstances have greater capacities to participate in achieving the greater good.

289. Those who willingly expand their positive experience have greater capacities to efficiently co-develop.

290. Those who control circumstances have more capacities of achieving more and greater successes.

291. Creative attitudes, qualities and capacities must be rewarded.

292. As we have more capacities and qualities, the more chances we have to meet several favorable occasions.

293. Ideas come fast and we forget them even faster. Ideas come out continuously, without us making any effort. Ideas that we seek, that we want to find we sometimes find them easily, other times very difficult and sometimes we can not fiind anything without looking   better.
Our ability to create ideas is a mine which can increase the value and on a continuous basis,   without   great   efforts.
Our ability to create ideas can continuously increase for as long as we live, thus increasing its value on a continuous basis. Our ability to create ideas affects us enormously in our achievement and

maintenance of our happiness every day in every situation.
One of the objectives of each personal man is necessary and should be the continuous development as much as the ability to create useful, efficient, positive, humane ideas, which can contribute to the achievement of our personal happiness and maintain it. As we grow with a grater ability to create positive, effective ideas, necessary to us, the more and more surely we can achieve personal goals and happiness and we can maintain them.
The ability to produce positive effective ideas, necessary to us is enormously useful and effective as it helps establish, develop, maintain other capacities as well which we can exemplify: 1) the ability to prevent mistakes and failures, 2) the ability to solve problems, 3) our ability to create and maintain happiness; 4) our ability to create, select, set and achieve personal goals; 5) our professional ability, 6) the ability to face any blows of life as big and as painful as they would be; 7) the ability to create and maintain a family, a happy marriage. The ability to produce positive effective ideas can increase greatly, easily and with

minimum expenditure, with the help of the Internet, knowledge, positive models, which we can find using the Internet. Until the creation and development of science and broadcasting them in an easy way for each, which includes the ability to create positive effective ideas, necessary to us, respectively the creation of science, the creativity of each of us, it is necessary to look in the edited books, in the media and on the Internet, whenever existing knowledge is needed.

Charming

294. Communication helps us become charming.

295. Our own happiness can be achieved and maintained also through the contribution of the formation, development, maintenance and usage of charming behavior.

296. We can prevent the falling apart of a happy marriage also through the contribution of the formation, development, maintenance and usage of charming behavior.

297. The necessary qualities in achieving personal goals can be formed, developed, maintained and used also through the

contribution of the formation, development, maintenance and usage of charming behavior.

298. Our happiness depends a lot also on the formation, development, maintenance and usage of charming behavior.

299. Rather than lamenting that we do not have successes it is more useful to also form, develop, maintain and use charming behavior.

300. In order to rise up once again for the first time for the who knows what time it is necessary to also form, develop, maintain and use charming behavior.

301. The force of our ideas can be augmented also through the contribution of the formation, development, maintenance and usage of charming behavior.

302. Stress can be prevented also through the formation, development, maintenance and usage of charming behavior.

303. Continuous self-motivation helps us become charming.

304. Pessimism can be removed and replaced with optimism also through the contribution of the formation, development, maintenance and usage of charming behavior.

305. We can become stronger and we can not allow ourselves to be influenced by the world also through the contribution of the formation, development, maintenance and usage of charming behavior.

306. The solutions to the problems we have or that we want to solve can be found also through the contribution of the formation, development, maintenance and usage of charming behavior.

307. Creativity helps us become charming.

308. We can overcome the difficulties that we must overcome also through the help of the formation, development, maintenance and usage of charming behavior.

309. Wisdom helps us become charming.

310. In order to escape poverty it is necessary to also form, develop, maintain and use charming behavior.

311. We can prevent some failures also through the contribution of the formation, development, maintenance and usage of charming behavior.

312. Responsibility helps us become charming.

313. The self efficient use of our time helps us become charming.

Communication

314. Communication helps us become charming.

315. Communication helps us become initiating.

316. Communication helps us become diplomatic.

317. Communication helps us become energetic.

318. Communication helps us become daring.

319. Communication helps us become rulers.

320. Communication helps us become bold.

321. Communication helps us become strong.

322. Communication helps us become decent.

323. Communication helps us become constant.

324. Communication helps us become meticulous.

325. Communication helps us become stimulating.

326. Communication helps us become expansive.

327. Communication helps us become funny.

328. Communication helps us become cultivated.

329. Communication helps us become popular.

330. Communication helps us become trained.

331. Communication helps us become selfless.

332. Communication helps us become convincing.

333. Communication helps us become self controlled.

334. Communication helps us become adaptable.

335. Communication helps us become animated.

336. Communication helps us become capable.

337. Communication helps us become sincere.

338. Communication helps us become positive.

339. Communication helps us become leaders.

340. Communication helps us become agreeable.

341. Communication helps us become attachable.

342. Communication helps us become good listeners.

343. Communication helps us become active.

Concentration

344. Permanent concentration on our personal objectives helps us achieve more efficient co operations.

345. Permanent concentration on our personal objectives helps us achieve more favorable situations.

346. Total concentration on personal goals helps us achieve more true friendships.

347. Permanent concentration on our personal objectives helps us achieve more pleasant surprises.

348. Total concentration on personal goals helps us achieve more performances.

349. Permanent concentration on our personal objectives helps us achieve more favorable chances.

350. Permanent concentration on our personal objectives helps us achieve more successes.

351. Total concentration on personal goals helps us achieve more pleasant surprises.

352. Permanent concentration on our personal objectives helps us achieve more personal goals.

353. Total concentration on personal goals helps us achieve more efficient co operations.

354. Total concentration on personal goals helps us achieve much good luck.

355. Permanent concentration on our personal objectives helps us achieve more performances.

356. Total concentration on personal goals helps us achieve more favorable situations.

357. Permanent concentration on our personal objectives helps us achieve much good luck.

358. Total concentration on personal goals helps us achieve more personal goals.

359. Permanent concentration on our personal objectives helps us achieve more true friendships.

360. Permanent concentration on our personal objectives helps us achieve more records.

361. Total concentration on personal goals helps us achieve more favorable chances.

362.	The increased capacity of concentration of our attention helps us and contributes to increasing our efficiency in what we do.

363.	To achieve quality actions to become happy and maintain our happiness, it is necessary that every time we act to focus totally on that action, to be careful in everything we do. Any little distraction can have grater or smaller negative effects on our happiness. Because of this, our happiness totally depends on our overall happiness and on the quality of actions which we achieve, on the concentration and attention with which we perform them.

Confidence

364.	Confidence in the idea that we can create our luck helps us achieve more efficient co operations.

365.	Confidence in the idea that we can create our luck helps us achieve more performances.

366.	Confidence in the success of what we do helps us achieve more records.

367.	Confidence in the success of what we do helps us achieve more efficient co operations.

368. Self confidence helps us achieve more successes.

369. Confidence in the idea that we can create our luck helps us achieve more favorable situations.

370. Confidence in the success of what we do helps us achieve more favorable chances.

371. Self confidence helps us achieve more performances.

372. Self confidence helps us achieve more true friendships.

373. Self confidence helps us achieve more pleasant surprises.

374. Confidence in the success of what we do helps us achieve more true friendships.

375. Self confidence helps us achieve more efficient co operations.

376. Confidence in the idea that we can create our luck helps us achieve more favorable chances.

377. Self confidence helps us achieve more favorable situations.

378. Self confidence helps us achieve much good luck.

379. Confidence in the success of what we do helps us achieve more successes.

380. Self confidence helps us achieve more favorable chances.

381. Confidence in the success of what we do helps us achieve much good luck.

382. Self confidence helps us achieve more records.

383. Confidence in the idea that we can create our luck helps us achieve more successes.

384. Confidence in the success of what we do helps us achieve more pleasant surprises.

385. Confidence in the idea that we can create our luck helps us achieve more records.

386. Confidence in the idea that we can create our luck helps us achieve more true friendships.

387. Confidence in the idea that we can create our luck helps us achieve more personal goals.

388. Confidence in the idea that we can create our luck helps us achieve much good luck.

389. Confidence in the success of what we do helps us achieve more favorable situations.

390. Confidence in the success of what we do helps us achieve more performances.

391. Confidence in the idea that we can create our luck helps us achieve more pleasant surprises.

392. Self confidence helps us achieve more personal goals.

393. A great capacity of increasing self confidence must be imitated.

394. A great capacity of maintaining self confidence helps us maintain our way of being loved.

395. Confidence in ourselves must be appreciated.

396. A great capacity of increasing self confidence helps us become enthusiastic.

397. A great capacity of increasing self confidence helps us become tolerant.

398. Confidence in ourselves helps us become understanding.

399. Confidence in ourselves helps us achieve much more pleasant surprises.

400. A great capacity of maintaining self confidence helps us become more productive.

401. A great capacity of maintaining self confidence helps us become understanding.

402. Confidence in ourselves helps us become energetic.

403. A great capacity of maintaining self confidence must be maintained.

404. A great capacity of maintaining self confidence helps us become more cautious.

Conflicts

405. Finding creative solutions that contribute to solving conflicts helps us achieve more records.

406. Preventing conflicts helps us achieve more personal goals.

407. Preventing conflicts helps us achieve more favorable chances.

408. The ability to solve conflicts helps us achieve more successes.

409. Preventing conflicts helps us achieve more successes.

410. Finding creative solutions that contribute to solving conflicts helps us achieve more favorable chances.

411. Finding creative solutions that contribute to solving conflicts helps us achieve more favorable situations.

412. Finding creative solutions that contribute to solving conflicts helps us achieve much good luck.

413. The ability to solve conflicts helps us achieve more favorable situations.

414. The art of solving conflicts helps us achieve more performances.

415. The ability to solve conflicts helps us achieve more pleasant surprises.

416. Preventing conflicts helps us achieve more true friendships.

417. Finding creative solutions that contribute to solving conflicts helps us achieve more successes.

418. The art of solving conflicts helps us achieve more true friendships.

419. The ability to solve conflicts helps us achieve much good luck.

420. The ability to solve conflicts helps us achieve more records.

421. The art of solving conflicts helps us achieve more records.

Correct

422. Our chances of becoming happy increase if we establish our personal goals correctly.

423. Our chances of becoming happy increase if we plan our actions correctly.

424. Our chances of becoming happy increase if we are correctly organize.

425. Successes in life can also be achieved thanks to the correct establishment of our personal goals.

426. Our way of seeing family relations, if it is correct helps us a lot to achieve a happy marriage.

427. Our way of seeing family relations can be correct or incorrect.

428. Our way of seeing love relations, if it is incorrect stops the achievement of true love.

429. Our way of seeing love relations, if it is correct helps us a lot to achieve a true love.

430. Our way of seeing love relations can be correct or incorrect.

431. Correct appreciations are appreciated a lot.

432. He who makes correct appreciations is esteemed by people.

433. He who makes correct appreciations is appreciated a lot by people.

434. People want to be appreciated correctly.

435. Illegal accusations can be prevented by effective laws and their correct application.

436. Mutual correct appreciations maintain friendships.

437. Those who see life in an incorrect way have a lot to suffer in life.

438. When we see life in an incorrect way it harms us a lot.

439. Developing our thinking can be achieved also through the formation, development, maintenance and usage of a correct life conception.

440. We can become stronger and we cannot let ourselves be influenced by the world also through the contribution of the formation, development, maintenance and usage of a correct life conception.

441. Correct thinking can be formed, developed and used also through the contribution of the formation, development, maintenance and usage of all only objective ideas.

Constructive

442. We can replace wrong ideas with correct ideas also through the contribution of the formation, development, maintenance and usage of constructive ideas.

443. Preventing the formation of doubts can be achieved also through the contribution of the formation, development, maintenance and usage of only constructive ideas.

444. Finding the meaning of our lives can be achieved also through the contribution of the formation, development, maintenance and usage of constructive thinking.

445. Those who do not think enough need to form, develop, maintain and use a constructive conception of life.

446. Emancipation from self imposed restrictions can be made through the formation, development, maintenance and usage of constructive thinking.

447. We can become stronger and we cannot let ourselves be influenced by the world also through the contribution of the formation, development, maintenance and usage of the

ability to solve problems only through constructive methods.

448. Our remaining in ignorance can be removed also through the contribution of the formation, development, maintenance and usage of a constructive conception of life.

449. Emancipation from self imposed restrictions can be made through the formation, development and maintenance of constructive thinking.

450. In order to change our desire of changing it is a really necessary that we form, develop, maintain and use constructive thinking.

451. We can prevent some mistakes also through the contribution of the formation, development, maintenance and usage of constructive ideas.

452. Pessimism can be removed and replaced with optimism also through the contribution of the formation, development, maintenance and usage of constructive thinking.

453. The desire to make others happy can be achieved through the contribution of the

formation, development, maintenance and usage of constructive thinking.

454. In order to pursue and transform our personal goals into reality we need to form, develop, maintain and use constructive thinking.

455. Constructive thinking helps us achieve only constructive behaviors.

456. We can broaden our horizon more or less also through the contribution of the formation, development, maintenance and usage of constructive thinking.

457. Those who do not think enough need to form, develop, maintain and use constructive thinking.

458. Problems cannot be solved by the ideas of that created them but also through the contribution of the formation, development, maintenance and usage of constructive behaviors.

459. Emancipation from self imposed restrictions can be made through the formation, development and maintenance of a great

ability to solve problems through constructive methods.

Character

460. Sometimes luck appears only because we have a character.

461. People who have had successes are people of character.

462. A responsible man is also a man of character.

463. A man's character can create many riches, but riches can not give back the character if it is lost.

464. Those who have as a personal objective the harmonious development of their character will succeed in life and achieve a more beautiful life than those who do not have among their personal goals the harmonious development of their personality.

465. Those who have as a personal objective the harmonious development of their character will succeed in life to achieve more successes and far fewer failures than those who do not have personal objectives and do not target their own harmonious development of their personality.

466. The man who has no good sense has no character.

467. Moral wealth is given by the moral character and values that each of us has.

Creativity

468. Creativity can be made more efficient.

469. Creativity must be maintained.

470. Creativity must be formed.

471. Creativity must be imitated.

472. Creativity must be used.

473. Creativity leads us to achieving greater or smaller successes.

474. Creativity helps us achieve more records.

475. Creativity helps us achieve true friendships.

476. Creativity helps us develop our qualities.

477. Creativity helps us form new qualities.

478. Creativity has multiple positive effects.

479. Creativity helps us achieve a happy marriage.

480. Creativity helps us achieve more personal goals.

481. Creativity helps us achieve more performances.

482. Creativity helps us achieve more efficient co operations.

483. Creativity helps us achieve more pleasant surprises.

484. Creativity helps us become expansive.

485. A great capacity of increasing creativity helps us become humane.

486. Creativity helps us become productive.

487. A great capacity of increasing creativity helps us become enthusiastic.

488. Creativity helps us become positive.

Credibility

489. Moral values continuously increase our credibility.

490. Solving problems through positive methods increases our credibility.

491. Those who discover unique ways to work efficiently for a better life increase their credibility.

492. A positive conception of life increases our credibility.

493. Long term thinking increases our credibility.

494. Constructive thinking increases our credibility.

495. Those who control circumstances increase their credibility.

496. Those who willingly expand their positive experience increase their credibility.

497. Efficient people in positive actions have more chances of increasing their credibility.

498. Those who know that discipline is one of the keys of dreams increased their credibility.

499. The sense of objectivity increases the credibility of the person who has it.

500. Sometimes the lack of common sense enormously reduces the credibility of the ones who do not have common sense.

501. Concentrating our energies increases our credibility.

502. A non hostile but aggressive behavior helps us increase our credibility.

503. People who are resistant to stress have a greater credibility.

504. Credibility many times brings us luck.

505. A positive enterprising spirit increases our credibility.

506. The sense of credibility helps us become more credible.

507. The sense of fairness increases our credibility.

508. Those who know how to take advantage of the opportunity to create increase their credibility.

509. Solving problems only through constructive methods increases our credibility.

Creative

510. Creative people are always young spirituals.

511. People who are always concerned about the future also have creative qualities.

512. Creative people have a futurological thought on a long term.

513. Creative people have a great capacity to create projects.

514. People can develop their creative potential for as long as they live.

515. The more creative qualities we have and the greater capacity of creation, the more we can find and discover more favorable circumstances for ourselves.

516. Creative ideas help us get performance.

517. It is necessary that we all contribute to forge a creative society.

518. The creative society makes everyone happier.

519. Creative people should be helped to create as much as possible.

520. The creative attitudes that we do not have we must form to help us become more creative.

521. The more creative we are, the greater capacity of creation we have, the more opportunities we have to meet several favorable occasions.

522. In life for as long as we live, it is necessary and useful to develop continuously, day by day, our creative skills and our creative abilities.

523. Our personal objective of the self-development of our creative skills, day by day, helps and contributes greatly to achieving our other personal objectives.

524. For as long as we live, continuously, day by day, it is necessary to have as a personal goal to form and develop as more creative qualities as we can.

525. How we live day by day, achieving the target of personal training and development of our creative skills helps and contributes greatly to achieving other personal objectives.

526. The more creative qualities we shape and develop, the more creative we become.

527. The orientation towards everything new is a creative attitude that helps us a lot to achieve personal goals.

528. If a person does not have creative attitude, a shift towards everything new, he can shape and develop it.

Daring

529. Optimism helps us become daring.

530. We can contribute to the achievement of our greatest accomplishments also through the contribution of the formation, development, maintenance and usage of daring behavior.

531. Positive experience can be achieved also through the contribution of the formation, development, maintenance and usage of daring behavior.

532. Release from our self-imposed restrictions can be made also through the contribution of the formation, development, maintenance and usage of daring behavior.

533. Confidence in ourselves helps us become daring.

534. In order to rise up once again for the first time for the who knows what time it is necessary to also form, develop, maintain and use daring behavior.

535. Acting efficiently helps us become daring.

536. The radical transformation for the better of our life can be achieved also through the

formation, development, maintenance and usage of daring behavior.

537. Self-imposed discipline helps us become daring.

538. In order to prevent failures it is necessary to also form, develop, maintain and use daring behavior.

539. The force of our ideas can be augmented also through the contribution of the formation, development, maintenance and usage of daring behavior.

540. Continuously making ourselves efficient helps us become daring.

541. We can overcome the difficulties that we must overcome also through the help of the formation, development, maintenance and usage of daring behavior.

542. Stress can be prevented also through the formation, development, maintenance and usage of daring behavior.

543. Responsibility helps us become daring.

544. Continuous self-motivation helps us become daring.

545. Obtaining more and greater successes can be achieved also through the contribution of the formation, development, maintenance, usage of a daring behavior.

546. Our future can be projected and achieved also through the contribution of the formation, development, maintenance and usage of daring behavior.

547. We can prevent the falling apart of a happy marriage also through the contribution of the formation, development, maintenance and usage of daring behavior.

Decisions

548. In order to trace and transform our personal objectives into reality it is necessary to form, develop, maintain and use the ability to take rapid quality decisions.

549. Obtaining more and greater successes can be achieved also through the contribution of the formation, development, maintenance and usage of a greater capacity to take rapid quality decisions.

550. In order to take correct decisions it is necessary to form, develop, maintain and use the ability to be responsible.

551. The ability to take rapid decisions increases our possibilities to prevent many unpleasant surprises.

552. The ability to take rapid decisions increases our chances to achieve efficient co-developments.

553. Young people need and must implicate themselves in taking all the decisions that affect them directly or indirectly.

554. The ability to take rapid decisions increases our capacity of achieving outstanding performances.

555. The ability to take rapid decisions increases our possibilities of achieving our personal goals a lot faster.

556. Most people who have had successes know how to take rapid decisions.

557. The ability of taking the rapid decisions increases our efficiency a lot.

Development

558. The obstacles that prevent us from achieving our personal goals can be surpassed also through the contribution of the formation, development, maintenance and usage of spontaneous behavior.

559. We can form, develop and maintain the state of being ourselves also through the contribution of the formation, development, maintenance and usage of a joyful behavior.

560. Positive experience can be achieved also through the contribution of the formation, development, maintenance and usage of a behavior with a theoretic spirit.

561. We can form, develop and maintain the state of being ourselves also through the contribution of the formation, development, maintenance and usage of a cheerful behavior.

562. We can contribute to the achievement of our greatest accomplishments also through the contribution of the formation, development, maintenance and usage of funny behavior.

563. We can overcome the difficulties that we must overcome also through the help of the

formation, development, maintenance and usage of bold behavior.

564.   Our own happiness can be achieved and maintained also through the contribution of the formation, development, maintenance and usage of analytic behavior.

565.   The radical transformation for the better of our life can be achieved also through the formation, development, maintenance and usage of sportive behavior.

566.   Positive experience can be achieved also through the contribution of the formation, development, maintenance and usage of bold behavior.

567.   Our own happiness can be achieved and maintained also through the contribution of the formation, development, maintenance and usage of charming behavior

568.   The radical transformation for the better of our life can be achieved also through the formation, development, maintenance and usage of leading behavior.

569.   Some mistakes can be prevented also through the contribution of the formation,

83

development, maintenance and usage of imaginative behavior.

Difficulties

570. We can overcome the difficulties that we must overcome also through the help of the formation, development, maintenance and usage of balanced behavior.

571. We can overcome the difficulties that we must overcome also through the help of the formation, development, maintenance and usage of inventive behavior.

572. We can overcome the difficulties that we must overcome also through the help of the formation, development, maintenance and usage of cheerful behavior.

573. We can overcome the difficulties that we must overcome also through the help of the formation, development, maintenance and usage of initiating behavior.

574. We can overcome the difficulties that we must overcome also through the help of the formation, development, maintenance and usage of agreeable behavior.

575. We can overcome the difficulties that we must overcome also through the help of the formation, development, maintenance and usage of efficient behavior.

576. We can overcome the difficulties that we must overcome also through the help of the formation, development, maintenance and usage of the loyal behavior.

577. We can overcome the difficulties that we must overcome also through the help of the formation, development, maintenance and usage of charming behavior.

578. We can overcome the difficulties that we must overcome also through the help of the formation, development, maintenance and usage of kind behavior.

579. We can overcome the difficulties that we must overcome also through the help of the formation, development, maintenance and usage of scientific spirit behavior.

580. We can overcome the difficulties that we must overcome also through the help of the formation, development, maintenance and usage of abstract behavior.

581. We can overcome the difficulties that we must overcome also through the help of the formation, development, maintenance and usage of intellectual behavior.

582. We can overcome the difficulties that we must overcome also through the help of the formation, development, maintenance and usage of logical behavior.

Discipline

583. Self-imposed discipline helps us become good listeners.

584. Self-imposed discipline helps us become altruistic.

585. Self-imposed discipline helps us become systematic.

586. Self-imposed discipline helps us become confident.

587. Self-imposed discipline helps us become independent.

588. In order to change into reality it is necessary to form, develop, maintain and use the sense of discipline.

589. Problems cannot be solved by the ideas that created them but also through the contribution of the formation, development, maintenance and usage of Self-imposed disciplined behaviors.

590. In order to change the desire of changing into reality it is necessary to form, develop, maintain and use the ability to self-impose the necessary discipline.

Disappointments

591. Getting out of the state of pessimism can be also achieved by studying theories on disappointments in psychology books.

592. Many of those who have no personal goals have lives that are full of trouble, sufferance, disappointments, failures, etc.

Discourage

593. The self-control of our behaviors helps us a lot to prevent discouragement.

594. Failures in friendships must never discourage us.

595. In order to pursue and transform our personal goals into reality we need to form

and develop the ability to be courageous and discouraged.

596. In order to trace and transform our personal goals into reality it is necessary that we form and develop the ability to form courage when we are discouraged.

597. Rather than being discouraged it is a lot better to search for solutions in solving the problems that we have.

598. A failure or failures should not discourage us.

599. Luxury should be discouraged.

600. Failures should never discourage us, because life also offers us many favorable situations to succeed. Through perseverance we will also find those favorable situations that will help us have success.

601. Any injustice that could be done to us should not discourage us.

602. If our objectives seem achievable to us, and many people consider them achievable without proof of evidence, their support should not discourage us.

603. Failures should never discourage us.

Differences

604. Sometimes something is won by small differences but the first, the winner also has 'n' more advantages than the second.

605. Discipline prevents differences.

606. The ability to solve differences helps us achieve more personal goals.

607. Finding creative solutions that contribute to solving differences helps us achieve more favorable situations.

608. The ability to solve differences helps us achieve much good luck.

609. Finding creative solutions that contribute to solving differences helps us achieve more pleasant surprises.

610. Finding creative solutions that contribute to solving differences helps us achieve more favorable chances.

611. The ability to solve differences helps us achieve more favorable chances.

612. Finding creative solutions that contribute to solving differences helps us achieve more personal goals.

613. The ability to solve differences helps us achieve more records.

614. The ability to solve differences helps us achieve more performances.

Dynamic

615. Good humor makes us more dynamic.

616. Love is a dynamic process, constantly transforming itself.

617. Those who are very active, dynamic, are more likely to encounter more favorable opportunities.

618. Hopes make us be more dynamic.

619. Luck runs into the one who is active, dynamic and industrious.

620. People who have success have a very dynamic behavior.

Eager

621. Release from our self-imposed restrictions can be made also through the contribution of the formation, development, maintenance and usage of a behavior eager for knowledge.

622. Our happiness depends a lot also on the formation, development, maintenance and usage of a behavior of being eager for knowledge.

623. We can overcome the difficulties that we must overcome also through the help of the formation, development.

624. Acting efficiently helps us become eager for knowledge.

625. Maintenance and usage of a behavior of being eager for knowledge.

626. Problems cannot be solved by the ideas that created them but also through the contribution of the formation, development, maintenance and usage of a behavior of being eager for knowledge.

627. Obtaining more and greater successes can be achieved also through the contribution of

the formation, development, maintenance, usage of a behavior eager for knowledge.

628. In order to prevent not achieving our personal goals, it is necessary to also form, develop, maintain and use our behavior of being eager for knowledge.

629. Our resistance to changing for the better can be overcome also through the contribution of the formation, development, maintenance and usage of a behavior eager for knowledge.

630. Aspiring towards a more meaningful life can also be achieved through the formation, development, maintenance and usage of a behavior of being eager for knowledge.

631. Stress can be prevented also through the formation, development, maintenance and usage of a behavior of being eager for knowledge.

632. Positive experience can be achieved also through the contribution of the formation, development, maintenance and usage of a behavior eager for knowledge.

Education

633. We can contribute to the achievement of our greatest accomplishments also through the contribution of the formation, development, maintenance and usage of continuous self-education behavior.

634. Successes in life can also be achieved thanks to continuous education.

635. Meanness is also the effect of the absence of our home education.

636. The meaning of life can be found through the contribution of the formation, development, maintenance and usage of self education.

637. Advanced education contributes sensibly to achieving a positive global future.

638. Advanced education contributes extensively to achieving more and greater successes.

639. Advanced education contributes extensively to achieving the future.

640. Educational needs change continuously and they must be satisfied immediately.

641. Humanist education reduces the insecurity of everyday life very much.

642. The education for humanist economy must take the place of the present economical education.

643. Permanent self education used in solving personal problems increases our trust in ourselves and in our possibilities.

644. Permanent self education helps us a lot to achieve more and greater successes.

645. An advanced education contributes greatly to achieving success in life.

646. Self- education for co-development is necessary to be a personal goal for each of us.

Efficiency

647. A great capacity of creating one's own safety helps us maintain our efficiency.

648. A great capacity of being flexible helps us maintain our efficiency.

649. Adaptation helps us maintain efficiency.

650. A great capacity of being as strong as possible helps us maintain our efficiency.

651. A great capacity of learning in order to achieve successes helps us maintain our efficiency.

652. A great capacity of appreciating people helps us maintain our efficiency.

653. A great capacity of learning how to achieve personal goals helps us maintain our efficiency.

654. A great capacity of using abilities helps us maintain our efficiency.

655. The desire to be grand helps us maintain our efficiency.

656. A great capacity of cherishing oneself helps us maintain our efficiency.

657. A great capacity of being tolerant with people helps us maintain our efficiency.

658. A great capacity of being honest with oneself helps us maintain our efficiency.

659. A great capacity of being creative in order to solve great problems helps us maintain our efficiency.

Enthusiasm

660. Those who are enthusiastic through their enthusiasm have a higher capacity to prevent many failures.

661. Those who are enthusiastic contribute through their enthusiasm to maintaining our health.

662. Those who are enthusiastic through their enthusiasm have greater chances to meet more favorable situations.

663. Optimism increases our enthusiasm.

664. Those who are enthusiastic have high chances to achieve a happy marriage with their enthusiasm.

665. Enthusiasm increases and maintains our perseverance.

666. An enthusiasm increases our power.

667. Optimism maintains our enthusiasm.

668. Personal goals also create enthusiasm.

669. Those who are enthusiastic become more credible through their enthusiasm.

670. The state of annoyance reduces our enthusiasm a lot.

671. The state of restlessness reduces a lot our enthusiasm.

672. The state of fatigue reduces a lot our enthusiasm.

673. Optimism creates enthusiasm.

674. True love increases our enthusiasm.

675. By orienting towards a future world we increase our enthusiasm.

676. In order to follow and transform our personal goals into reality, it is necessary to also form, develop, maintain and use our enthusiasm.

677. A great capacity of anticipating helps us maintain our enthusiasm.

678. A great capacity of using available ideas helps us maintain our enthusiasm.

679. A great capacity of using a value system helps us maintain our enthusiasm.

680. A great capacity of being honest with oneself helps us maintain our enthusiasm.

681. A great capacity of using abilities helps us maintain our enthusiasm.

Ethical

682. Ethical principles help us a lot in achieving our personal goals.

683. Ethical principles help us a lot in achieving more and greater successes.

684. Ethical principles help us form and develop efficient co-developments.

Exceptional

685. Imagination is a main factor that helps us a lot to deal with exceptional difficult situations.

686. In 2007 the behaviors of the majority of people in the world are mostly selfish behaviors unfortunately. They are very harmful because these behaviors are particularly concerned with the interests of his own people, irrespective of the account that they damage other people and in some cases, exceptional people even die or huge damages are made.

687. True friendship is tested in exceptionally difficult situations.

688. Some successes are due only to the qualities and exceptional efforts of people without the participation of any favorable circumstances.

689. In 2007, in most people in the world most behaviors are selfish behaviors unfortunately, they are very harmful ones because such behaviors are concerned with in particular, the interests of their own persons, irrespective of the fact that they often harm other people and in some exceptional cases people even die, or have huge damages.

690. True friends are those who wish you well, cooperate with you when you need to, who are there by your side in every good and bad situation. They are those people who do not leave in exceptional circumstances, the most difficult ones of your life.

Experience

691. The daily gathering of as much experience as possible helps us achieve more pleasant surprises.

692. The daily gathering of as much experience as possible helps us achieve much good luck.

693. The daily gathering of as much experience as possible helps us achieve more true friendships.

694. The daily gathering of as much experience as possible helps us achieve more efficient co operations.

695. The daily gathering of as much experience as possible helps us achieve more records.

696. The daily gathering of as much experience as possible helps us achieve more personal goals.

697. The daily gathering of as much experience as possible helps us achieve more favorable chances.

698. Positive experience can be achieved also through the contribution of the formation, development, maintenance and usage of a behavior with a theoretic spirit.

699. Positive experience can be achieved also through the contribution of the formation,

development, maintenance and usage of bold behavior.

700. Positive experience can be achieved also through the contribution of the formation, development, maintenance and usage of respectful behavior.

701. Positive experience can be achieved also through the contribution of the formation, development, maintenance and usage of agreeable behavior.

702. Positive experience can be achieved also through the contribution of the formation, development and maintenance of the ability to efficiently organize our time.

703. By using experience we develop efficient collaborations.

704. We can achieve objectives through experience.

705. Failure can be prevented by taking as an example the experience of others.

706. Positive experience can be achieved also through the contribution of the formation, development and maintenance of the ability to be calm in stressing situations.

Facing

707. A great capacity of facing one's own life must be a model.

708. A great capacity of facing one's own life must be developed.

709. A great capacity of facing one's own life helps us achieve more favorable chances.

710. A great capacity of facing one's own life helps us maintain our way of being liked.

711. In life, it is necessary to allow ourselves to be influenced only by positive influences, and when facing potential negative influences we must be immune.

712. Those who have the ability of facing mental stress have more chances and a higher potential to achieve their desired future.

713. A great capacity of facing one's own life helps us become more loved.

714. A great capacity of facing one's own life helps us become practical.

715. A great capacity of facing one's own life helps us maintain our tolerance.

716. A great capacity of facing one's own life helps us maintain our happiness.

717. A great capacity of facing one's own life helps us maintain our efficiency.

718. A great capacity of facing one's own life helps us become more pleasant.

719. A great capacity of facing one's own life helps us become more preventive.

720. A great capacity of facing one's own life helps us maintain our way of being understanding.

Feelings

721. When people reveal their feelings mutually they contribute a lot to maintaining inter-human relations.

722. When friends reveal their feelings mutually they contribute a lot to maintaining a true friendship.

723. Spouses must reveal their feelings mutually.

724. Feelings must be rewarded with feelings.

725. Feelings must be appreciated.

726. Feelings must be expressed.

727. Our happiness depends on the power to control our feelings.

728. People who have had successes mostly have envious feelings.

729. Each of us must have the strength and willpower to prevent negative feelings, to maintain and develop happiness because they are extremely harmful for us and for others.

730. Negative feelings damage us and others. Attention not to make them, maintain and develop them.

731. In life it is necessary and required to develop only positive feelings just because they only do us and others good.

732. People who have deep feelings are also sensitive and profound.

733. Each of us has the strength and will, if we want, to prevent the happiness, maintaining and development of negative feelings because they are extremely harmful to to us and others.

734. Negative feelings harm both us and the others. Beware not to form, maintain and develop them.

735. In life it is necessary and required to develop positive feelings just because they only do us and others good.

736. By developing their inner beauty, the qualities, skills, abilities and feelings that make them happy, women can create more joy and satisfactions.

Forming

737. Forming, developing and rewarding positive performance in children makes us not have performers in negative performance, namely criminals.

738. Love is a dynamic process, constantly transforming itself.

739. Self imposed discipline helps us and contributes a lot to forming social relations.

740. Forming, developing and using more and more qualities helps us prevent the situation of reaching despair.

741. Forming and developing harmonious global co-development thinking in an accelerated rhythm most certainly leads to solving many problems of mankind.

742. Creative thinking contributes a lot to forming, developing and promoting harmonious global co-development thinking.

743. Although forming and developing a creative thinking helps us achieve our personal objectives many of us do not use it.

744. The activity of voluntarism can help us a lot in forming and developing our qualities.

745. Continuous self perfection increases our potential of becoming more performing.

746. The sense of responsibility contributes a lot to forming and developing our trust in the future.

747. Quality actions help us and contribute a lot in forming and developing co-developments.

748. By doing the right thing we will succeed in forming a corresponding thinking to success.

749. Consciousness helps us become more performing.

750. Forming and developing co-development thinking must be for each of us a personal goal.

751. Some people with wrong ideas cannot become more performing because of their wrong ideas.

752. People with prejudice may not become more performing because of some prejudices.

753. Assuring personal freedom contributes to and helps us become more performing.

754. Those who know how to take advantage of the opportunity to create have more chances to become more performing.

755. People who are skilled become more performing.

756. The sense of commitment in work helps us a lot to become more performing.

757. People who inspire trust have a greater ability to become more performing.

758. Those who discover unique ways to work efficiently for a better life become more performing.

759. The sense of quality helps us become more performing.

760. Those who willingly express their positive experience continuously increase their ability of becoming more performing.

761. People who do not have hopes of creating other hopes need to connect with people who have succeeded in forming their trust in the future.

762. Those who have not succeeded in forming a happy marriage up to a certain date need to form and develop their sense of fairness in order to succeed.

763. People who have not succeeded in forming a happy marriage up to a certain date need to form and develop their own value system in order to succeed.

764. People who have not succeeded in achieving a happy marriage up to a certain day need to form and develop their ability of forming and developing the strategies of achieving happiness in order to succeed.

765. People who have not succeeded in forming a happy marriage up to a certain time need

to form and develop their ability of achieving more and greater successes in order to succeed.

766. All of those who have not succeeded in forming a happy marriage up to a certain date need to form and develop their ability of achieving true friendships in order to succeed.

767. A better organization makes us more performing.

Fairness

768. The sense of fairness increases our chances to achieve a mature love.

769. The sense of fairness increases our credibility.

770. The sense of fairness helps us become more effective.

771. The sense of fairness helps us achieve positive performances.

772. The sense of fairness increases our chances to achieve a more beautiful life.

773. The sense of fairness increases our chances to achieve efficient co-developments.

774. The sense of fairness helps us achieve a happy life.

775. Those who do not have hopes of creating hope in the future need to form their sense of fairness.

776. Those who have not succeeded in forming a happy marriage up to a certain date need to form and develop their sense of fairness in order to succeed.

777. Fairness sometimes brings us to luck.

778. We can overcome the difficulties that we need to overcome also through the formation, development and maintenance of the sense of fairness in everything we do.

779. Forming wrong ideas can be prevented also through the formation, development, maintenance and usage of the sense of fairness.

780. Those who have high objectives in life mostly have the sense of fairness.

781. People with human social behaviors need to have the sense of fairness.

782. People who know how to prevent possible mistakes mostly have the sense of fairness.

783. Persons who have the ability to react with understanding also have the sense of fairness.

Flexibility

784. Flexibility increases our chances of achieving more objectives.

785. Flexibility increases our chances of achieving more successes.

786. In order to transform positive objectives into reality it is necessary to form, develop, maintain and use the sense of flexibility.

787. The limits we have set can be overcome by the formation, development, maintenance and usage of the sense of flexibility.

788. Emancipation from restrictions can be made through the formation, development and maintenance of the sense of flexibility.

789. Forming wrong ideas can be prevented also through the formation, development, maintenance and usage of flexibility.

790. People who have had successes have the sense of flexibility.

791. Those who have high objectives in life mostly have the sense of flexibility.

792. Flexibility increases our chances of achieving true friendships.

793. Flexibility helps us a lot to achieve more and greater successes.

794. Flexibility increases our chances to meet more favorable situations.

795. Flexibility in thinking and behaviors can be learned from those who have it.

796. Flexibility in thinking and behaviors is a quality necessary to achieve personal goals.

797. Flexibility in thinking and behaviors can be formed and developped if we do not have it.

798. Flexibility in thinking and behaviors helps us surpass many hard to overcome obstacles.

799. Flexibility in thinking and behavior helps us achieve much easier, much faster and a larger number of personal goals.

Focus

800. Keeping the focus on achieving personal goals helps us achieve more successes.

801. Keeping the focus on achieving personal goals helps us achieve more favorable chances.

802. In order to pursue and transform our personal goals into reality we need to form, develop, maintain and use the ability to focus.

803. Focusing on what we do helps us a lot to have even more chances to meet more favorable situations.

804. The state of restlessness reduces a lot our ability to focus.

805. Focusing on what we do helps us make the things we do of good quality.

806. Focusing on what we do helps us a lot to achieve personal goals.

807. When we focus on what we are doing we increase our chances to prevent mistakes.

808. Focusing on what we do is a necessity.

809. A nervous state reduces a lot our capacity to focus.

810. The increased ability to focus our attention helps us contribute greatly to achieving more fulfillments.

811. Increasing the ability to focus attention helps us and contributes to achieving independence.

812. Increasing the ability to focus our attention helps contribute to the increasing of our efficiency in what we do.

Friendship

813. Preventing everything that harms women helps us achieve more true friendships.

814. Preventing accidents helps us achieve more true friendships.

815. Finding creative solutions to the problems helps us achieve more true friendships.

816. The art of solving arguments helps us achieve more true friendships.

817. Openness towards new solutions helps us achieve more true friendships.

818. The power of hope helps us achieve more true friendships.

819. The faithfulness of collaborators helps us achieve more true friendships.

820. The attitude of not letting ourselves be stopped helps us achieve more true friendships.

821. Passion for our work helps us achieve more true friendships.

822. Imitating positive deeds helps us achieve more true friendships.

823. The desire to be efficient helps us achieve more true friendships.

824. Total concentration on personal goals helps us achieve more true friendships.

825. Preventing failures helps us achieve more true friendships.

826. Preventing everything that harms young people helps us achieve more true friendships.

827. Useful ideas help us achieve more true friendships.

828. Our positive attitude towards life helps us achieve more true friendships.

829. Rising from more failures helps us achieve more true friendships.

830. Preventing the inefficient use of resources helps us achieve more true friendships.

831. Knowing about changes helps us achieve more true friendships.

832. Those who have a good behavior help us achieve more true friendships.

Giving

833. Never giving up helps us achieve more performances.

834. Never giving up helps us achieve more favorable chances.

835. Never giving up helps us achieve much good luck.

836. Never giving up helps us achieve more personal goals.

837. Forgiving is a wise behavior.

838. Forgiving is a positive behavior.

839. Very giving people, who are ready to interrupt their own way in order to help others, are an engine of global humanization.

840. Very giving people, who are ready to interrupt their own way in order to help others, are an engine of development in each area of activity.

841. People who are forgiving are also good.

842. People who are forgiving are admired, esteemed, respected and rewarded.

843. People who are forgiving manage to achieve true friendships.

844. People who are forgiving know how to maintain a true mature love.

845. Before giving an answer to a question it is necessary that one thinks about the answer and not give an answer without thinking.

846. The majority of people who have successes are giving.

847. By giving the attention and time necessary to nourish our souls we increase our chances to achieve personal goals.

848. Very giving persons who are willing to interrupt their own way in order to help others, have greater chances to achieve efficient co operations.

849. Very giving people ready to interrupt their own road to help others have the potential to become more efficient.

850. Very giving people ready to interrupt their own road to help others have greater chances to achieve a more beautiful life.

Goals

851. Preventing conflicts helps us achieve more personal goals.

852. The power of continuously being effective helps us achieve more personal goals.

853. The passion of achieving personal goals helps us achieve more efficient co operations.

854. Prevention against bad people helps us achieve more personal goals.

855. The desire to become even more effective helps us achieve more personal goals.

856. Preventing the inefficient use of the resources of informatics helps us achieve more personal goals.

857. The passion of achieving personal goals helps us achieve much good luck.

858. Keeping the focus on achieving personal goals helps us achieve more successes.

859. Setting high personal goals helps us achieve more personal goals.

860. Preventing inefficiencies helps us achieve more personal goals.

861. Total concentration on personal goals helps us achieve more true friendships.

862. Loving what we do helps us achieve more personal goals.

863. Discovering true instincts helps us achieve more personal goals.

864. The passion of achieving personal goals helps us achieve more pleasant surprises.

865. Making problems aware helps us achieve more personal goals.

866. Total concentration on personal goals helps us achieve more performances.

867. Our loyalty helps us achieve more personal goals.

Habits

868. We must permanently form effective habits.

869. Efficient habits help us achieve a happy life.

870. Effective habits help us obtain our own successes.

871. Positive habits can be developed continuously.

872. We can form positive habits.

873. Life is a lot easier if we have only positive habits.

874. Those who fail to escape the routine of everyday habits have inefficient behavior, are messy, slow, chaotic, etc. and they will have many failures and few and small achievements in life.

875. Routine and daily habits should not be a brake for us, an impassable barrier in the

form of our other more efficient, more orderly, faster, etc. behaviors.

876. Routine and daily habits should not be a brake for us, an impassable barrier in the form of our other more efficient, more orderly, faster, etc. behaviors

Happiness

877. The desire to be grand helps us maintain our happiness.

878. Our own happiness can be achieved and maintained also through the contribution of the formation, development, maintenance and usage of impersonal behavior.

879. Our happiness depends a lot also on the formation, development, maintenance and usage of adaptable behavior.

880. Our happiness depends a lot also on the formation, development, maintenance and usage of balanced behavior.

881. Our happiness depends a lot also on the formation, development, maintenance and usage of analytic behavior.

882. Our own happiness can be achieved and maintained also through the contribution of the formation, development, maintenance and usage of analytic behavior.

883. Our own happiness can be achieved and maintained also through the contribution of the formation, development, maintenance and usage of charming behavior.

884. Our happiness depends a lot also on the formation, development, maintenance and usage of joyful behavior.

885. Our own happiness can be achieved and maintained also through the contribution of the formation, development, maintenance and usage of continuous self perfecting behavior.

886. Our own happiness can be achieved and maintained also through the contribution of the formation, development, maintenance and usage of sensible behavior.

887. A great capacity of being wise helps us maintain our happiness.

888. Our happiness depends a lot also on the formation, development, maintenance and usage of conscientious behavior.

Harmonious

889. When friends sense each other they have more chances to achieve harmonious relations.

890. When people sense each other they have more chances to achieve harmonious relations.

891. Those without hopes for the future need to become friends with those who harmoniously develop their personality.

892. People who have had successes mostly know how to harmoniously develop their personality.

893. Those who do not have hopes, in order to create hopes for the future they need to connect with people who have harmoniously developed their personality.

894. Efficient positive human communication contributes a lot to achieving harmonious social relations.

895. Those who are preoccupied with creating an optimal cooperation in the team contribute a lot to creating a harmonious climate.

896. Working in teams of people with similar values is harmonious.

897. A man who has practical values usually knows how to harmoniously develop his personality.

898. A realistic man in everything he does knows how to harmoniously develop his personality.

Hope

899. Release from self imposed restrictions can also be made through the formation, development and maintenance of hopes.

900. People who do not have hopes, in order to create hopes need to connect with people who have the ability to face mental stress.

901. Most of those involved in many projects have more hopes that increase their chances of participating in many efficient global co operations.

902. Long term thinking creates many hopes.

903.   Most of those who have not succeeded in forming a happy marriage up to a certain date need to form and develop the abilities of creation, development and maintenance of hopes.

904.   Persons who do not have hopes, in order to create hopes for the future they need to connect with people who have the ability to take rapid decisions.

905.   People with no hopes for the future need to connect with those who have the ability of rapid perception.

906.   Those who do not have hopes, in order to create hopes for the future, they need to get themselves involved in relations with people who have the sense of fairness.

907.   Obtaining as many and great successes that we can, can be achieved through the contribution of formation, development, maintenance and usage of the ability to form, develop and maintain hopes.

908.   Aspirations toward a more meaningful life can be achieved also through the contribution of the formation, development,

maintenance and usage of the ability to create, develop and maintain hopes.

909. Emancipation from self imposed restrictions can be made through the formation, development and maintenance of hopes.

910. Hopes can be created also through the contribution of the formation, development, maintenance and usage of a behavior of continuous self-motivation.

Honest

911. A great capacity of being honest with oneself helps us achieve more favorable chances.

912. A great capacity of being honest with oneself helps us become more practical.

913. A great capacity of being honest with oneself helps us maintain our way of being loving.

914. A great capacity of being honest with oneself helps us become happier.

915. A great capacity of being honest with oneself helps us maintain our tolerance.

916. A great capacity of being honest with oneself helps us maintain our way of being liked.

917. A great capacity of being honest with oneself helps us become more efficient.

918. A great capacity of being honest with oneself helps us achieve more personal goals.

919. A great capacity of being honest with oneself helps us achieve more performances. A great capacity of being honest with oneself helps us become enthusiastic.

920. A great capacity of being honest with oneself helps us become efficient.

921. In order to follow and transform our personal goals into reality, it is necessary to also form, develop, maintain and use our honest behavior.

922. True friendships rely on honesty.

923. Honesty demands honesty.

924. An honest woman has more chances to achieve a happy marriage.

925. Troubles can be prevented through using honest behaviors.

926. People who have had successes are mostly honest.

927. An honest man manages to earn his living in life.

928. An honest man works hard all the time.

929. Honest men must be promoted, supported, appreciated.

930. An honest man is consistent in honest behaviors.

931. Those who are very honest are much appreciated.

932. An honest man is appreciated, respected and esteemed by other people.

933. Honesty brings us luck.

934. Those who establish as an objective to be honest and continuously act with commitment to achieve this objective will be honest.

Honorable

935. Perseverant people are honorable.

936. Perseverance gives us power, strenghtens us, makes us honorable, respected and appreciated.

937. People with successes are honorable.

Hypocrisy

938. Hypocrisy harms the hypocrite one very much.

939. Hypocrisy makes those who are hypocrites be rejected by others.

940. A strong man by his hypocrisy enormously damages himself due to his hypocrisy.

941. He who is hypocritical only has common sense to achieve his hypocrisy.

942. Hypocrisy only creates problems and nothing positive.

943. Hypocrisy alienates others from the hypocritical one.

944. Hypocrisy is extremely dangerous.

945. He who is hypocrite through his hypocrisy enormously harms himself because of his hypocrisy.

946. The hypocrisy of a friend towards the other leads to the destruction of the friendship.

947. Hypocrisy can not be found between two friends.

948. Hypocrisy is a defect that harms people very much.

949. Hypocrisy is a big flaw that harms us very much in life.

Ideals

950. Our life's transformation for the better can be achieved if we have ideals.

951. People with high ideals have much greater chances of achieving efficient co operations.

952. Those who are remarkably gifted mostly have a lot of ideals.

Immorality

953. Immorality is a question of many misfortunes.

954. Immorality is a factor of many failures.

955. Immorality undermines the very immoral one.

956. Immorality makes the immoral ones be rejected by others.

957. Immorality is enormously harmful to society.

Ignorance

958.   Ignorance can be fought by using discipline.

959.   Our ignorance can be removed by progressive conceptions of life.

960.   Our remaining in ignorance can be eliminated also through the contribution of the formation, development, maintenance and usage of progressive ideas.

961.   Our remaining in ignorance can be eliminated also through the contribution of the formation, development, maintenance and usage of a constructive conception of life.

962.   Ignorance can be avoided through creativity and study.

963.   Our remaining in ignorance can be removed also through the contribution of the formation, development, maintenance and usage of a positive life conception.

964.   Our remaining in ignorance can be removed also through the contribution of the formation, development, maintenance and usage of creative sense.

965. Our remaining in ignorance can be removed also through the contribution of the formation, development, maintenance and usage of a legal conception of life.

966. Our remaining in ignorance can be removed also through the contribution of the formation, development, maintenance and usage of the ability to make the positive necessary changes in our personal life.

967. Our remaining in ignorance can be removed also through the contribution of the formation, development, maintenance and usage of an efficient conception of life.

968. Our remaining in ignorance can be removed also through the contribution of the formation, development, maintenance and usage of a constructive conception of life.

969. Our remaining in ignorance can be removed also through the contribution of the formation, development, maintenance and usage of a realistic life conception.

970. Our remaining in ignorance can be removed also through the contribution of the formation, development, maintenance and usage of progressive ideas.

971. Our remaining in ignorance can be removed also through the contribution of the formation, development, maintenance and usage of a constructive life conception.

972. Our remaining in ignorance can be removed also through the contribution of the formation, development, maintenance and usage of scientific thinking.

973. Remaining in a state of ignorance can be fought through the contribution of the formation, development, maintenance and usage of a positive life conception.

974. Ignorance is the cause of many failures.

975. Ignorance is a cause of pessimism.

976. Ignorance is the cause of many divorces.

977. Ignorance is the cause of many mistakes.

978. Ignorance is the cause of many arguments.

979. Ignorance also produces envy.

980. Ignorance produces much evil.

981. Meanness is a result of ignorance.

982. Sometimes ignorance makes our life very complicated.

Indecision

983. Indecision can sometimes harm us very much.

984. When we are doubtful we must find solutions to get rid of indecision.

985. Indecision is the cause of many casualties.

986. Indecision is the cause of many accidents.

987. Indecision is the cause of many failures.

Inefficinent

988. Preventing the inefficient use of the resources of informatics helps us achieve more efficient co operations.

989. Preventing the inefficient use of financial resources helps us achieve much good luck.

990. Preventing the inefficient use of the resources of informatics helps us achieve more personal goals.

991. Preventing the inefficient use of human resources helps us achieve more records.

992. Preventing the inefficient use of financial resources helps us achieve more successes.

993. Preventing the inefficient use of material resources helps us achieve much good luck.

994. Preventing the inefficient use of resources helps us achieve more true friendships.

995. Preventing the inefficient use of financial resources helps us achieve more true friendships.

996. Preventing the inefficient use of financial resources helps us achieve more records.

997. Preventing the inefficient use of the resources of informatics helps us achieve more favorable chances.

998. Preventing the inefficient use of the resources of informatics helps us achieve more performances.

999. Preventing the inefficient use of material resources helps us achieve more personal goals.

1000. Preventing the inefficient use of resources helps us achieve more successes.

1001. Preventing the inefficient use of human resources helps us achieve more favorable chances.

1002. Preventing the inefficient use of financial resources helps us achieve more personal goals.

Influence

1003. A great capacity of having one's own principles and not letting one be influenced by the negative opinions of others helps us maintain our way of being cautious.

1004. We can become stronger and we can not allow ourselves to be influenced by the world also through the contribution of the formation, development, maintenance and usage of sturdy behavior.

1005. We can become stronger and we can not allow ourselves to be influenced by the world also through the contribution of the formation, development, maintenance and usage of ingenious behavior.

1006. We can become stronger and we can not allow ourselves to be influenced by the world also through the contribution of the formation, development, maintenance and usage of astute behavior.

1007. We can become stronger and we can not allow ourselves to be influenced by the world also through the contribution of the formation, development, maintenance and usage of daring behavior.

1008. A great capacity of having one's own principles and not letting one be influenced by the negative opinions of others helps us maintain our optimism.

1009. We can become stronger and we can not allow ourselves to be influenced by the world also through the contribution of the formation, development, maintenance and usage of diplomatic behavior.

1010. We can become stronger and we can not allow ourselves to be influenced by the world also through the contribution of the formation, development, maintenance and usage of idealistic behavior.

1011. A great capacity of having one's own principles and not letting one be influenced by the negative opinions of others helps us become practical.

1012. We can become stronger and we can not allow ourselves to be influenced by the world also through the contribution of the formation, development, maintenance and usage of productive behavior.

1013. We can become stronger and we can not allow ourselves to be influenced by the world also through the contribution of the formation, development, maintenance and usage of profound behavior.

1014. A great capacity of having one's own principles and not letting one be influenced by the negative opinions of others must be encouraged.

1015. A great capacity of having one's own principles and not letting one be influenced by the negative opinions of others helps us become more loving.

1016. A great capacity of having one's own principles and not letting one be influenced by the negative opinions of others helps us become more tolerant.

1017. A great capacity of having one's own principles and not letting one be influenced by the negative opinions of others helps us become more enthusiastic.

1018. A great capacity of having one's own principles and not letting one be influenced by the negative opinions of others helps us maintain our way of being understanding.

1019. We can become stronger and we can not allow ourselves to be influenced by the world also through the contribution of the formation, development, maintenance and usage of ordered behavior.

1020. We can become stronger and we can not allow ourselves to be influenced by the world also through the contribution of the formation, development, maintenance and usage of sociable behavior.

1021. A great capacity of having one's own principles and not letting one be influenced by the negative opinions of others helps us become tolerant.

1022. A great capacity of having one's own principles and not letting one be influenced by the negative opinions of others helps us achieve more true friendships.

1023. We can become stronger and we can not allow ourselves to be influenced by the world also through the contribution of the formation, development, maintenance and usage of sincere behavior.

Ingenuity

1024. Ingenuity must be recognized.

1025. Ingenuity must be appreciated.

1026. Ingenuity is a creative quality.

1027. Our ingenuity helps us create and maintain a happy family.

Initiatives

1028. Assuming initiatives helps us achieve much good luck.

1029. Assuming initiatives helps us achieve more favorable situations.

1030. Assuming initiatives helps us achieve more favorable chances.

1031. Assuming initiatives helps us achieve more successes.

1032. Assuming initiatives helps us achieve more records.

1033. Assuming initiatives helps us achieve more personal goals.

1034. Assuming initiatives helps us achieve more pleasant surprises.

1035. Assuming initiatives helps us achieve more true friendships.

1036. The financing by the state of more positive, efficient initiatives, helpful to people and society should contribute a lot and would accelerate the development of their personality, their integration into society, from participating in the realization of many activities of society.

1037. The state's funding of more positive and effective initiatives, useful for the youth and for society would greatly reduce the number of young negative facts.

1038. Countries should promote, encourage and finance more positive and effective initiatives of young people.

Innovating

1039. People with an innovating spirit have a great potential to participate in efficient global co operations.

1040. People with and innovating spirit have much more chances to meet more favorable situations.

1041. People with an innovating spirit more easily achieve efficient co operations.

1042. People with an innovating spirit more easily achieve social relations.

1043. People who have an innovating spirit have more potential to find the right partner for life.

1044. People who have and innovating spirit have more potential to increase their efficiency.

Intelectual

1045. The force of our ideas can be augmented also through the contribution of the formation, development, maintenance and usage of intellectual behavior.

1046. We can prevent the falling apart of a happy marriage also through the contribution of the formation, development, maintenance and usage of intellectual behavior.

1047. Our future can be projected and achieved also through the contribution of the formation, development, maintenance and usage of intellectual behavior.

1048. In order to prevent not achieving our personal goals, it is necessary to also form, develop, maintain and use our intellectual behavior.

1049. Acting efficiently helps us become intellectual.

1050. The radical transformation for the better of our life can be achieved also through the formation, development, maintenance and usage of intellectual behavior.

1051. In order to escape poverty it is necessary to also form, develop, maintain and use intellectual behavior.

1052. Positive experience can be achieved also through the contribution of the formation, development, maintenance and usage of intellectual behavior.

1053. Our own happiness can be achieved and maintained also through the contribution of the formation, development, maintenance and usage of intellectual behavior.

1054. Our resistance to changing for the better can be overcome also through the contribution of the formation, development, maintenance and usage of intellectual behavior.

1055. In order to prevent failures it is necessary to also form, develop, maintain and use intellectual behavior.

1056. Release from our self-imposed restrictions can be made also through the contribution of the formation, development, maintenance and usage of intellectual behavior.

Irresponsability

1057. Unfortunately there are still enormously many people in functions with high responsibilities but who unfortunately prove much irresponsibility.

1058. After a while, when they are divorced, they realize their irresponsibility, the enormous value that they had lost and that their children had lost.

1059. Leaders of countries have an enormous responsibility to the people, but unfortunately they often demonstrate very much and great irresponsibility.

1060. All employees of international organizations and states, which act during the performance of their duties with irresponsibility should be dismissed immediately and effective measures to recover the damage created by their irresponsible actions should be taken.

1061. The irresponsibility of many people stopped in a lot of ways until now, progress in many areas.

Joyful

1062. Our future can be projected and achieved also through the contribution of the formation, development, maintenance and usage of joyful behavior.

1063. We can form, develop and maintain the state of being ourselves also through the contribution of the formation, development, maintenance and usage of a joyful behavior.

1064. The radical transformation for the better of our life can be achieved also through the formation, development, maintenance and usage of joyful behavior.

1065. Our happiness depends a lot also on the formation, development, maintenance and usage of joyful behavior.

1066. Problems cannot be solved by the ideas that created them but also through the contribution of the formation, development, maintenance and usage of joyful behavior.

1067. We can contribute to the achievement of our greatest accomplishments also through the contribution of the formation, development, maintenance and usage of joyful behavior.

1068. Continuously making ourselves efficient helps us become joyful.

1069. In order to escape poverty it is necessary to also form, develop, maintain and use joyful behavior.

1070. Hopes can be created also through the contribution of the formation, development, maintenance and usage of joyful behavior.

1071. The force of our ideas can be augmented also through the contribution of the formation, development, maintenance and usage of joyful behavior.

1072. Our own happiness can be achieved and maintained also through the contribution of the formation, development, maintenance and usage of joyful behavior.

1073. We can prevent the falling apart of a happy marriage also through the contribution of the formation, development, maintenance and usage of joyful behavior.

1074. Continuous self perfection helps us become joyful.

Kind

1075. Continuous self-control helps us become kind.

1076. In order to rise up once again for the first time for the who knows what time it is necessary to also form, develop, maintain and use kind behavior.

1077. In order to rise up once again for the first time for the who knows what time it is necessary to also form, develop, maintain and use kind behavior.

1078. Optimism helps us become kind.

1079. Will helps us become kind.

1080. The self efficient use of our time helps us become kind.

1081. The force of our ideas can be augmented also through the contribution of the formation, development, maintenance and usage of kind behavior.

1082. We can form, develop and maintain the state of being ourselves also through the contribution of the formation, development, maintenance and usage of a kind behavior.

1083. Problems cannot be solved by the ideas that created them but also through the contribution of the formation, development, maintenance and usage of kind behavior.

1084. Wisdom helps us become kind.

1085. Some mistakes can be prevented also through the contribution of the formation, development, maintenance and usage of kind behavior.

1086. Positive experience can be achieved also through the contribution of the formation, development, maintenance and usage of kind behavior.

1087. We can overcome the difficulties that we must overcome also through the help of the formation, development, maintenance and usage of kind behavior.

1088. Stress can be prevented also through the formation, development, maintenance and usage of kind behavior.

1089. Pessimism can be removed and replaced with optimism also through the contribution of the formation, development, maintenance and usage of kind behavior.

1090. The solutions to the problems we have or that we want to solve can be found also through the contribution of the formation, development, maintenance and usage of kind behavior.

1091. Acting efficiently helps us become kind.

1092. Release from our self-imposed restrictions can be made also through the contribution of the formation, development, maintenance and usage of kind behavior.

1093. Our own happiness can be achieved and maintained also through the contribution of the formation, development, maintenance and usage of kind behavior.

1094. Rather than lamenting that we do not have successes it is more useful to also form, develop, maintain and use kind behavior.

Kindness

1095. In order to follow and transform our personal goals into reality, it is necessary to also form, develop, maintain and use our kindness.

1096. Kindness must never lack.

Knowledge

1097. The daily gathering of as much useful knowledge as possible helps us achieve more efficient co operations.

1098. Gaining useful knowledge every day helps us achieve more records.

1099. The daily gathering of as much useful knowledge as possible helps us achieve more performances.

1100. The daily gathering of as much useful knowledge as possible helps us achieve much good luck.

1101. Gaining useful knowledge every day helps us achieve much good luck.

1102. The daily gathering of as much useful knowledge as possible helps us achieve more records.

1103. The daily gathering of as much useful knowledge as possible helps us achieve more pleasant surprises.

1104. Gaining useful knowledge every day helps us achieve more pleasant surprises.

1105. The daily gathering of as much useful knowledge as possible helps us achieve more favorable chances.

1106. Gaining useful knowledge every day helps us achieve more successes.

1107. The daily gathering of as much useful knowledge as possible helps us achieve more favorable situations.

1108. The daily gathering of as much useful knowledge as possible helps us achieve more successes.

1109. The daily gathering of as much useful knowledge as possible helps us achieve more personal goals.

1110. Gaining useful knowledge every day helps us achieve more favorable chances.

1111. Gaining useful knowledge every day helps us achieve more performances.

1112. The daily gathering of as much useful knowledge as possible helps us achieve more true friendships.

1113. A great capacity of using available knowledge helps us become more efficient.

1114. Release from our self-imposed restrictions can be made also through the contribution of the formation, development, maintenance and usage of a behavior eager for knowledge.

1115. A great capacity of using available knowledge helps us become more cautious.

1116. Our happiness depends a lot also on the formation, development, maintenance and usage of a behavior of being eager for knowledge.

1117. We can overcome the difficulties that we must overcome also through the help of the formation, development, maintenance and usage of a behavior of being eager for knowledge.

1118. Acting efficiently helps us become eager for knowledge.

Laziness

1119. Laziness brings only suffering.

1120. Laziness stops those who are lazy from getting a job.

1121. Laziness makes many people poor.

1122. Laziness is a dangerous defect.

1123. Laziness a dangerous defect.

1124. Laziness has never led to the achievement of any success.

1125. Laziness makes people who are lazy be put on the lists of dismissals.

1126. Laziness has never led to anything.

1127. Laziness of one of the spouses is likely to lead to divorce.

1128. Laziness is a cause of poverty for many poor people.

1129. Laziness also makes us even poorer.

1130. Laziness leads us to poverty.

Learning

1131. Learning from other people's mistakes helps us achieve more favorable situations.

1132. Learning how to solve problems helps us achieve more records.

1133. Learning how to solve problems helps us achieve much good luck.

1134. Learning from other people's mistakes helps us achieve more successes.

1135. Learning how to solve problems helps us achieve more performances.

1136. A great capacity of learning how to achieve personal goals helps us achieve more performances.

1137. A great capacity of learning in order to achieve successes helps us maintain our optimism.

1138. A great capacity of learning in order to achieve successes must be supported.

1139. A great capacity of learning how to achieve personal goals helps us become productive.

1140. A great capacity of learning in order to achieve successes helps us achieve more personal goals.

1141. A great capacity of learning how to achieve personal goals must be maintained.

1142. A great capacity of learning how to achieve personal goals must be rewarded.

1143. A great capacity of learning how to achieve personal goals helps us become practical.

1144. A great capacity of learning how to achieve personal goals helps us maintain our tolerance.

1145. A great capacity of learning how to achieve personal goals helps us maintain our efficiency.

1146. A great capacity of learning how to achieve personal goals must be developed.

1147. The quality of learning effectively must be formed if we do not have it.

1148. Self-imposed discipline can be obtained through experiences, through practice, through imitating, through learning, etc.

1149. The quality of learning how to learn helps us form the abilities we lead to achieve our personal goals.

1150. The quality of learning how to learn increases our chances to be more efficient.

1151. The quality of learning how to learn helps us become more operative.

Long-term

1152. The effects of human actions have an increasing influence on the environment. This makes us think on a global scale, long-term and scientific before acting and makes us perform more profound studies, of impact, regarding our actions, to prevent the implementation of actions that have negative, inadmissible effects on the environment, society and people.

1153. To have the least possible number of failures in our life it is also necessary to have a long-term thinking.

1154. We can prevent many failures can with the help of long-term thinking.

1155. Thinking long-term helps us to prevent many mistakes.

1156. We can prevent a very large number of inefficient actions with a long-term thinking.

1157. Incredible facts are made mostly by people who have long-term objectives and work with dedication to achieve them.

1158. Long-term thinking is specific to futurological thinking.

1159. Hopes make us form our long-term thinking.

1160. Thinking long-term helps and contributes greatly to increasing our confidence in us.

1161. A man with a broad horizon most of the times has a long-term thinking.

1162. People with human social behaviors have a long-term thinking.

1163. People with no hopes for the future need to connect with those who have a long-term thinking.

1164. In order to escape poverty it is necessary to form, develop, maintain and use long-term thinking.

1165. Hopes can be created by using a long-term thinking.

Love

1166. A great capacity of positively influencing people helps us become loved.

1167. A great capacity of assuming the necessary risks for success helps us maintain our way of being loved.

1168. Our resistance to changing for the better can be overcome also through the contribution of the formation, development, maintenance and usage of a behavior of being in love with life.

1169. A great capacity of maintaining self confidence helps us maintain our way of being loved.

1170. In achieving our successes a contribution is also brought by the formation, development, maintenance and usage of a behavior of being in love with life.

1171. A great capacity of gathering our energies helps us become loved.

1172. A great capacity of being convincing helps us maintain our way of being loved.

1173. A great capacity of working hard helps us become loved.

1174. A great capacity of drawing attention helps us maintain our way of being loved.

1175. A great capacity of forming a positive own lifestyle helps us become more loved.

1176. Positive experience can be achieved also through the contribution of the formation, development, maintenance and usage of a behavior of being in love with life.

1177. A great capacity of continuously overcoming boundaries helps us become more loved.

Loyalty

1178. The loyalty of friends helps us achieve much good luck.

1179. Our loyalty helps us achieve more favorable situations.

1180. Our loyalty helps us achieve more favorable chances.

1181. Our loyalty helps us achieve more personal goals.

1182. The loyalty of friends helps us achieve more pleasant surprises.

1183. The loyalty of friends helps us achieve more efficient co operations.

1184. Our loyalty helps us achieve more performances.

1185. Our loyalty helps us achieve much good luck.

1186. The loyalty of friends helps us achieve more successes.

1187. The loyalty of friends helps us achieve more records.

1188. Our loyalty helps us achieve more pleasant surprises.

1189. Loyalty creates psychical comfort.

1190. Loyalty must be repaid with loyalty.

1191. Loyalty also demands loyalty.

1192. Loyalty is a quality and value used to maintain a mature love.

1193. Loyalty is a quality and value used to maintain true friendship.

1194. Loyalty is a quality and value used to maintain a happy marriage.

1195. Loyalty to the company increases if employees are motivated and rewarded non-financially as well.

1196. Non-financial rewards along with increased financial rewards motivate employees and thier loyalty.

1197. Loyalty is a factor of many true friends.

1198. Loyalty is a factor of many successes.

1199. Loyalty is a factor of many lasting friends.

1200. Loyalty is a factor of many sustainable co operations.

Long-lasting

1201. Happy long-lasting marriages have many positive effects.

1202. Friendly behavior helps us create long-lasting loves.

1203. Friendly behavior helps us create long-lasting marriages.

1204. Friendly behavior helps us create long-lasting friendships.

1205. Friendly behavior helps us create long-lasting co operations.

Mannered

1206. In order to prevent failures it is necessary to also form, develop, maintain and use mannered behavior.

1207. Continuous self perfection helps us become mannered.

1208. Our own happiness can be achieved and maintained also through the contribution of the formation, development, maintenance and usage of mannered behavior.

1209. The solutions to the problems we have or that we want to solve can be found also through the contribution of the formation, development, maintenance and usage of mannered behavior.

1210. The obstacles that prevent us from achieving our personal goals can be surpassed also through the contribution of the formation, development, maintenance and usage of mannered behavior.

1211. We can form, develop and maintain the state of being ourselves also through the contribution of the formation, development, maintenance and usage of a mannered behavior.

1212. In order to escape poverty it is necessary to also form, develop, maintain and use mannered behavior.

1213. The force of our ideas can be augmented also through the contribution of the formation, development, maintenance and usage of mannered behavior.

1214. Communication helps us become mannered.

1215. Our future can be projected and achieved also through the contribution of the formation, development, maintenance and usage of mannered behavior.

1216. Pessimism can be removed and replaced with optimism also through the contribution of the formation, development, maintenance and usage of mannered behavior.

1217. Rather than lamenting that we do not have successes it is more useful to also form, develop, maintain and use mannered behavior.

1218. Wisdom helps us become mannered.

1219. In order to rise up once again for the first time for the who knows what time it is necessary to also form, develop, maintain and use mannered behavior.

1220. The limits of achievement imposed by ourselves in our mind at a given moment can be overcome or eliminated also through the contribution of the formation, development, maintenance and usage of mannered behavior.

1221. Hope helps us become mannered.

Misunderstandings

1222. The ability to solve misunderstandings helps us achieve more pleasant surprises.

1223. Finding creative solutions that contribute to solving misunderstandings helps us achieve more true friendships.

1224. The art of solving misunderstandings helps us achieve more true friendships.

Model

1225. A great capacity of making great plans must be a model.

1226. A great capacity of adopting visions must be a model.

1227. The dream to the grand must be a model.

Moral

1228. Moral values continuously increase our credibility.

1229. Moral values help us a lot in maintaining effective co operations.

1230. Moral values make us more credible.

1231. Moral values help us a lot to achieve effective co operations.

1232. Moral values create most of the times great masterpieces.

1233. Good morale helps us very much to achieve effective co operations.

1234. Good morale helps us very much in achieving records.

1235. Good morale helps us a lot to us achieve personal goals.

1236. Good morale helps us greatly to achieve a greater efficiency.

1237. Good morale needs to be kept constant, every day, for as long as we live.

1238. An optimal morale increases our chances of not reaching panic situations.

1239. An optimal morale can be formed through a proper diet, education, intellectual exercises, perseverance, will, physical exercises, etc.

1240. An optimal morale increases our chances of not reaching the situations of despair.

1241. Self education helps us form an optimal morale.

1242. An optimal morale helps us achieve an efficient development.

1243. Physical beauty without moral beauty sometimes destroys itself.

1244. A journalist who knowingly, for some reward, misinforms private citizens has no moral right to be a journalist, but also because legally his facts are crimes.

1245. There are men who appreciate more the moral beauty than the physical beauty of a woman.

1246. The moral beauty of a woman complements her natural beauty and makes her more attractive.

1247. Natural beauty without a moral one sometimes self-destroys.

1248. A judge who made a single injustice, has no moral right to judge. What to say to those who do daily tens of deeds of injustice, or annually thousands of deeds of injustice?

Mistakes

1249. Learning from other people's mistakes helps us achieve more favorable situations.

1250. Preventing mistakes helps us achieve much good luck.

1251. Learning from the others' mistakes helps us achieve more efficient co operations.

1252. Learning from other people's mistakes helps us achieve more performances.

1253. Preventing mistakes helps us achieve more pleasant surprises.

1254. Preventing mistakes helps us achieve more favorable chances.

1255. Learning from the others' mistakes helps us achieve more pleasant surprises.

1256. Learning from other people's mistakes helps us achieve more personal goals.

1257. Learning from our mistakes helps us achieve more efficient co operations.

1258. Learning from the others' mistakes helps us achieve much good luck.

1259. Learning from other people's mistakes helps us achieve more true friendships.

1260. Learning from our mistakes helps us achieve more favorable chances.

1261. Learning from other people's mistakes helps us achieve more successes.

1262. Learning from the others' mistakes helps us achieve more records.

1263. Learning from the others' mistakes helps us achieve more successes.

1264. Learning from the others' mistakes helps us achieve more performances.

1265. Learning from the others' mistakes helps us achieve more favorable chances.

Motivate

1266. In order to pursue and transform positive objectives into reality it is necessary to form and develop the ability to know how to motivate people.

1267. Obtaining as many and greatest successes as we can, can be achieved through the formation, development and maintenance of the ability to motivate people.

1268. Positive experience can be achieved also through the contribution of the formation, development and maintenance of the ability to efficiently motivate people.

1269. By listening very carefully to what people who have had successes say and by taking useful ideas from them we can form, develop, maintain and use the ideas of that help us motivate ourselves.

1270. We can contribute to achieving our happiness also through the contribution of the formation, development, maintenance and usage of the ability to motivate ourselves.

1271. Obstacles that stop us from achieving our personal goals can be overcome also through the contribution of the formation, development, maintenance and usage of ideas that motivate others.

1272. We can prevent some mistakes also through the formation of the formation, development, maintenance and usage of the ability to motivate ourselves.

1273. People with human social behaviors have a great ability to motivate people.

1274. People who have had successes mostly have known how to motivate people.

1275. People who want to obtain success must form and develop the ability to motivate people.

1276. Persons who have not succeeded in forming a happy marriage up to a certain date, in order to succeed they need to develop the ability of knowing how to motivate.

1277. People who do not have hopes, in order to create hopes for the future, need to connect with people who know how to motivate people.

1278. Efficient people in positive actions must be motivated.

1279. Those who know how to take quality decisions form and develop the ability to motivate people.

1280. In order to change your desire of changing it is really necessary to form, develop, maintain and use the ability to efficiently motivate people.

Meaningful

1281. Aspiring towards a more meaningful life can also be achieved through the formation, development, maintenance and usage of strong behavior.

1282. Aspiring towards a more meaningful life can also be achieved through the formation, development, maintenance and usage of a behavior of being devoid of prejudices.

1283. Aspiring towards a more meaningful life can also be achieved through the formation, development, maintenance and usage of continuous self motivating behavior.

1284. Aspiring towards a more meaningful life can also be achieved through the formation, development, maintenance and usage of ingenious behavior.

1285. Aspiring towards a more meaningful life can also be achieved through the formation, development, maintenance and usage of continuous control of the self behavior.

1286. Aspiring towards a more meaningful life can also be achieved through the formation, development, maintenance and usage of constant behavior.

1287. Aspiring towards a more meaningful life can also be achieved through the formation, development, maintenance and usage of a behavior of being in a good mood.

1288. Aspiring towards a more meaningful life can also be achieved through the formation, development, maintenance and usage of sturdy behavior.

1289. Aspiring towards a more meaningful life can also be achieved through the formation, development, maintenance and usage of flexible behavior.

1290. Aspiring towards a more meaningful life can also be achieved through the formation, development, maintenance and usage of firm behavior.

1291. Aspiring towards a more meaningful life can also be achieved through the formation, development, maintenance and usage of vivacious behavior.

1292. Aspiring towards a more meaningful life can also be achieved through the formation, development, maintenance and usage of reasonable behavior.

1293. Aspiring towards a more meaningful life can also be achieved through the formation, development, maintenance and usage of continuous self-controlling behavior.

1294. Aspiring towards a more meaningful life can also be achieved through the formation, development, maintenance and usage of understanding behavior.

1295. Aspiring towards a more meaningful life can also be achieved through the formation, development, maintenance and usage of stimulating behavior.

1296. Aspiring towards a more meaningful life can also be achieved through the formation, development, maintenance and usage of optimistic behavior.

1297. Aspiring towards a more meaningful life can also be achieved through the formation, development, maintenance and usage of continuous self perfecting behavior.

Mentalities

1298. Negative mentalities of those who have them slow the achievement of effective co operations.

1299. Negative mentalities of those who have them greatly slow the achievement of personal goals.

1300. Those with negative mentalities do not achieve effective co-developments.

1301. Negative mentalities make it very hard to do effective actions.

1302. Negative mentalities make it very hard for us to achieve successes.

1303. Negative mentalities for those who do not prevent them keep them from having some successes that they could achieve.

1304. If you unfortunately have some negative mentalities (which may be crimes) it is better to stop using them.

1305. Some behaviors, called mentalities, are not in fact mentalities, but crimes.

1306. Negative mentalities make those who prevent them deserving to have some successes.

1307. If you unfortunately have some negative mentalities (which may be crimes) is good to stop their use.

1308. The negative mentalities of those who have them make it very difficult to achieve efective co operations.

1309. The negative mentalities of those who have them make it very difficult to achieve personal goals.

Methods

1310. We can prevent some mistakes through the contribution of the formation, development, maintenance and usage of the capacity to solve problems only through constructive methods.

1311. In order to pursue and transform positive objectives into reality it is necessary to form, develop, maintain and use the ability to solve problems only the constructive methods.

1312. The ability to solve problems through positive methods keeps us away from the negative implication of the world.

1313. Forming wrong ideas can be prevented through the contribution of the formation, development, maintenance and usage of the ability to solve problems only through positive methods.

1314. The state of psychical discomfort can be removed through the formation, development and maintenance of the ability to solve problems through positive methods.

1315. Our negative transformation can be avoided through the formation, development, maintenance and usage of the ability to solve problems only through positive methods.

1316. In order to pursue and transform positive objectives into reality it is necessary to form, develop, maintain and use the ability to solve problems through positive methods.

1317. Emancipation from restrictions can be made through the formation, development and maintenance of a great ability to solve problems through positive methods.

1318. In order to pursue and transform our personal goals into reality we need to form, develop, maintain and use the ability to solve problems only through positive methods.

1319. Emancipation from self imposed restrictions can be made through the formation, development and maintenance of a great ability to solve problems through constructive methods.

1320. Obtaining as many and great successes that we can can be achieved through the contribution of formation, development, maintenance and usage of the ability to solve a problem through constructive methods.

1321. Obtaining as many and great successes that we can can be achieved through the contribution of formation, development, maintenance and usage of a great ability to solve problems through positive methods.

Meticulous

1322. The limits of achievement imposed by ourselves in our mind at a given moment can be overcome or eliminated also through the contribution of the formation, development, maintenance and usage of meticulous behavior.

1323. Obtaining more and greater successes can be achieved also through the contribution of the formation, development, maintenance, usage of a meticulous behavior.

1324. Positive experience can be achieved also through the contribution of the formation, development, maintenance and usage of meticulous behavior.

1325. Optimism helps us become meticulous.

1326. Continuous self perfection helps us become meticulous.

1327. We can prevent the falling apart of a happy marriage also through the contribution of the formation, development, maintenance and usage of meticulous behavior.

1328. Release from our self-imposed restrictions can be made also through the contribution of the formation, development, maintenance and usage of meticulous behavior.

1329. Creativity helps us become meticulous.

1330. Stress can be prevented also through the formation, development, maintenance and usage of meticulous behavior.

1331. Cherishing oneself helps us become meticulous.

1332. Self-imposed discipline helps us become meticulous.

1333. The obstacles that prevent us from achieving our personal goals can be surpassed also through the contribution of the formation, development, maintenance and usage of meticulous behavior.

1334. We can prevent some failures also through the contribution of the formation, development, maintenance and usage of meticulous behavior.

1335. Problems cannot be solved by the ideas that created them but also through the contribution of the formation, development, maintenance and usage of meticulous behavior.

1336. In order to rise up once again for the first time for the who knows what time it is necessary to also form, develop, maintain and use meticulous behavior.

1337. We can become stronger and we can not allow ourselves to be influenced by the world also through the contribution of the formation, development, maintenance and usage of meticulous behavior.

Necessary

1338. Greed is necessary to be detested.

1339. It is necessary for normality to take the place of abnormality.

1340. Periodic analysis of our actions is very necessary to help us increase the effectiveness of future actions.

1341. Literacy is necessary for every man of the planet.

1342. Selflessness is a model of positive behavior that is necessary to appreciate.

1343. If we have single children up to 18 years it is necessary for both parents to do everything they can not to divorce.

1344. If we have children, in order to prevent divorce and its negative effects, it is necessary for scientists to pay more attention to studying family relationships and family.

1345. The effective management of our time is a necessary quality.

1346. If we think how much is necessary for every action that we want to do, we can prevent many mistakes.

1347. It is necessary to apply any useful idea as soon as possible.

1348. In achieving our objectives it is necessary to find and use effectively all the possibilities.

1349. Preventive thinking is extremely necessary.

1350. Patience is a special and necessary quality.

1351. We have the opportunity to make peace at any time; it is necessary that we do it.

1352. It is necessary at all times to develop our human qualities.

1353. When the future seems desperate it is necessary to study books on positive thinking.

Nervosity

1354. The state of nervosity makes it very hard to achieve our own happiness.

1355. The state of nervosity stops the achievement of efficient co-developments.

1356. The state of nervosity stops us from achieving outstanding performances.

1357. The state of nervosity makes it hard to achieve true friendships.

1358. The state of nervosity makes it very hard to maintain efficient co operations.

1359. The state of nervosity makes it very hard to achieve personal goals.

1360. The state of nervosity stops us from solving problems through constructive methods.

1361. The state of nervosity makes it very hard to maintain social relations.

1362. The state of nervosity stops us from becoming more credible.

1363. The state of nervosity continues to create many problems in relations of cooperation.

1364. The state of nervosity continues to create stress in the family life.

1365. The state of nervosity continues to push people away from us.

1366. The state of nervosity makes it very hard to succeed in life.

Neglected

1367. Today's knowledge can help us greatly to achieve a much happier life. Unfortunately most of this knowledge is neglected.

1368. There are many divorces, the only reason for that, banal at first glance, is that spouses have neglected marital sex. Do not forget the sex lecture. Do not neglect domestic sex.

1369. He who is neglected in work makes many mistakes.

1370. Each woman has the need not to be neglected.

Objective

1371. Permanent concentration on our personal objectives helps us achieve more favorable situations.

1372. Permanent concentration on our personal objectives helps us achieve more pleasant surprises.

1373. Permanent concentration on our personal objectives helps us achieve more favorable chances.

1374. Permanent concentration on our personal objectives helps us achieve more successes.

1375. Permanent concentration on our personal objectives helps us achieve more personal goals.

1376. Permanent concentration on our personal objectives helps us achieve more performances.

1377. A great capacity of remaining involved in the same area with even greater objectives helps us maintain our tolerance.

1378. A great capacity of remaining involved in the same area with even greater objectives helps us maintain our enthusiasm.

1379. A great capacity of remaining involved in the same area with even greater objectives must be maintained.

1380. A great capacity of remaining involved in the same area with even greater objectives must be appreciated.

1381. A great capacity of remaining involved in the same area with even greater objectives helps us achieve more favorable situations.

1382. A great capacity of remaining involved in the same area with even greater objectives helps us become more efficient.

1383. A great capacity of remaining involved in the same area with even greater objectives helps us become understanding.

1384. In order to pursue and transform positive objectives into reality it is necessary to form, develop, maintain and use the ability to be oriented towards long lasting successes.

1385. In order to pursue and transform positive objectives into reality it is necessary to form, develop, maintain and use the ability to make the necessary positive changes in our professional life.

1386. In order to pursue and transform positive objectives into reality it is necessary to form, develop, maintain and use the ability to create unique ways to work efficiently for a better life.

1387. In order to pursue and transform positive objectives into reality it is necessary to form, develop, maintain and use the ability to make the necessary positive changes in our personal life.

1388. In order to pursue and transform positive objectives into reality it is necessary to form, develop, maintain and use the ability to achieve, develop, and maintain human social behaviors.

1389. In order to pursue and transform positive objectives into reality it is necessary to form, develop, maintain and use the ability to solve old problems.

Objectivity

1390. The desire to make others happy can be accomplished through the contribution of the formation, development, maintenance and usage of the sense of social objectivity.

1391. Those who have the sense of objectivity have more and greater chances to achieve a more beautiful life.

1392. The sense of objectivity increases the credibility of the person who has it.

1393. Those who have the sense of objectivity have more and greater chances to achieve a happy life.

1394. Those who have the sense of objectivity have the capacity to maintain efficient co-developments.

1395. Those who have the sense of objectivity make many exchanges of information.

1396. Those who have the sense of objectivity have contributed a lot in achieving the greater good.

1397. Those with the sense of objectivity have more and greater chances to achieve a true mature love.

1398. Those with the sense of objectivity must be rewarded.

1399. Those with the sense of objectivity have greater chances to achieve efficient co operations.

1400. Those who have the sense of objectivity have more and greater chances to achieve outstanding performances.

1401. Those with the sense of objectivity have more and greater chances to prevent more failures.

1402. Those with the sense of objectivity contribute a lot to global humanization.

1403. Those with the sense of objectivity must be appreciated.

1404. Those with the sense of objectivity have more and greater chances to meet more favorable situations.

1405. Those with the sense of objectivity have more chances to achieve social relations.

1406. Those with the sense of objectivity have more and higher chances to achieve their own happiness.

Obstacles

1407. The obstacles that prevent us from achieving our personal goals can be surpassed also through the contribution of the formation, development, maintenance and usage of spontaneous behavior.

1408. The obstacles that prevent us from achieving our personal goals can be surpassed also through the contribution of the formation, development, maintenance and usage of unpretentious behavior.

1409. The obstacles that prevent us from achieving our personal goals can be surpassed also through the contribution of the formation, development, maintenance and usage of continuous self-controlling behavior.

1410. The obstacles that prevent us from achieving our personal goals can be surpassed also through the contribution of the formation, development, maintenance and usage of loyal behavior.

1411. The obstacles that prevent us from achieving our personal goals can be surpassed also through the contribution of the formation, development, maintenance and usage of continuous effective usage of our time behavior.

1412. Positive imagination helps us a lot to overcome many obstacles.

1413. Obstacles can be surpassed and eliminate it through the formation, development, maintenance and usage of the ability to support others.

1414. Obstacles that stop us from achieving our objectives can be removed by the ability to perfect ourselves.

1415. Obstacles that stop us from achieving our personal goals can be overcome also through the contribution of the formation, development, maintenance and usage of the ability to solve problems legally.

1416. Obstacles that stop us from achieving our personal goals can be overcome also through the contribution of the formation, development, maintenance and usage of a constructive behavior.

1417. The obstacles that prevent us from achieving our personal goals can be surpassed also through the contribution of the formation, development, maintenance and usage of analytic behavior.

1418. The obstacles that prevent us from achieving our personal goals can be surpassed also through the contribution of the formation, development, maintenance and usage of calm behavior.

1419. The obstacles that prevent us from achieving our personal goals can be surpassed also through the contribution of the formation, development, maintenance and usage of reasonable behavior.

1420. The obstacles that prevent us from achieving our personal goals can be surpassed also through the contribution of the formation, development, maintenance and usage of leadership behavior.

Optimism

1421. Optimism is one of the weapons that obtain successes.

1422. Success creates optimism.

1423. Successes create optimism.

1424. Optimism is a factor of many successes.

1425. Many times optimism is contagious.

1426. Optimism help us a lot to us achieve a more beautiful life.

1427. Failures should never defeat our optimism.

1428. Hopes are creators of optimism.

1429. Optimism helps us achieve performances.

1430. Optimism helps us get rid of stress.

1431. Optimism prevents us from reaching the state of despair.

1432. Optimism helps us increase our chances of achieving a more beautiful live.

1433. A good state of health contributes a lot to maintaining our optimism.

1434. Optimism increases our chances very much to achieve true friendships.

1435. A nervous state reduces our optimism.

1436. Optimism helps us get through life's difficulties a lot easier.

1437. Self delusion reduces our optimism.

1438. Discipline maintains optimism.

1439. Optimism leads us towards successes.

1440. Optimism helps us a lot and increases our chances to achieve a happy marriage.

1441. An optimistic man through his optimism motivates people.

1442. Optimism is an advantage in front of hardship.

1443. Optimism increases the chances of achieving more efficient co-developments.

1444. Optimism is the state that helps us obtain more and greater successes.

1445. Optimism increases are possibilities of achieving a mature love.

1446. An optimistic man has succeeded in building the achievements on his optimism.

1447. The state of restlessness reduces a lot our optimism.

1448. The state of fatigue reduces a lot our optimism.

1449. Optimism helps us a lot to increase our chances and prevent stress.

1450. Pessimism can be removed and replaced with optimism also through the contribution of the formation, development, maintenance and usage of positive thinking.

1451. Those who have not succeeded to achieve a happy marriage up to a certain date need to form and develop the ability of forming and developing strategies of formation, development and maintenance of optimism.

1452. Pessimism can be removed and replaced with optimism also through the contribution of the formation, development, maintenance and usage of the long term thinking.

1453. Pessimism can be removed and replaced with optimism also through the contribution of the formation, development, maintenance and usage of the ability to achieve the necessary efficient co operations.

1454. Pessimism can be removed and replaced with optimism also through the contribution of the formation, development, maintenance and usage of creative thinking.

1455. Pessimism must be replaced with optimism in any situation.

1456. We can eliminate pessimism and replace it with optimism also through the contribution of the formation, development, maintenance and usage of optimistic ideas.

1457. Desperation can be eliminated also through the contribution of the formation, development, maintenance and usage of optimism.

Open-minded

1458. People who have had successes are mostly open-minded.

1459. Communicative people are more open-minded.

Operative

1460. The documentation necessary to achieve the personal goals we need, we can complete from existing books or with the help of the Internet, in a very effective, cheap and operative way, etc..

1461. An intelligent man is cooperative in activities.

1462. Our hostile non aggressive behavior helps us become more operative.

1463. Co-development makes us become more cooperative with other people in other situations.

1464. Cooperative behavior helps us have more opportunities to meet more favorable circumstances.

1465. Cooperative behavior helps us have more opportunities to co-develop.

1466. Cooperative behavior helps us have more opportunities to achieve more efficient co operations and with more people.

1467. Non-cooperative employees are the first on the list of dismissals.

1468. Co- development makes us become more cooperative with other people in other situations.

1469. The effective management of our time helps us become much more efficient and operative.

1470. The man who is cooperative in activities has greater chances to prevent more failures.

1471. People who are cooperative in activities can contribute a lot to global humanization.

1472. A man who is cooperative during activities must be promoted, supported and rewarded.

1473. A man who is cooperative during activities has more chances to participate in efficient global co operations.

1474. A positive operative spirit increases our ability to achieve mature love.

1475. A positive operative spirit increases our ability to have more and greater chances to meet more and greater favorable situations.

1476. A positive operative spirit makes us commit fewer mistakes.

1477. A positive operative spirit increases our ability to achieve more and greater successes.

1478. A positive operative spirit creates the possibility to become more efficient.

1479. A cooperative man in activities has more possibilities of achieving more social relations.

1480. A cooperative man in activities has a greater potential of achieving his personal goals.

1481. Team spirit helps us become more cooperative.

1482. The quality of learning how to learn helps us become more operative.

1483. A cooperative man in activities is more available to the exchange of information.

1484. A cooperative man in activities more easily achieves efficient co-developments.

Positive

1485. Positive ideas should be always taken into account.

1486. Positive ideas are the engines of progress.

1487. Positive ideas should be storaged in idea banks.

1488. Positive actions surely take us to larger or smaller successes, even if we realize them with bigger or smaller efforts.

1489. Behavior for luxury can be prevented by positive thinking.

1490. Selflessness is a model of positive behavior that is necessary to appreciate.

1491. Positive facts have multiple positive effects.

1492. Positive facts should be valued.

1493. Positive actions should be taken as models.

1494. Positive actions prevent many negative actions.

1495. Positive actions should be appreciated.

1496. Supporting positive action is a necessity.

1497. Through positive actions we can prevent many failures.

1498. We can prevent sorrows through a positive thinking.

1499. By acting continuously and effectively to achieve positive goals we will surely achieve them.

1500. Many problems can be avoided by thinking positive.

1501. Positive tips are a resource to our happiness.

1502. Some positive special facts create heroes.

1503. The more idols we have the more necessary it is that all our behaviors be positive.

1504. Successes are also effects of positive thinking.

1505. Objectivity is essential to positive action.

1506. Positive thinking prevents much harm.

1507. By having a positive thinking we can prevent many mistakes.

1508. Positive ideas should be promoted as much as possible.

1509. Positive ideas are the only ideas that help us and contribute to the achievement of personal goals.

1510. Positive ideas help us achieve successes.

1511. Positive ideas should be supported to take the place of negative ideas.

1512. We must create the conditions so that sociable people achieve their objectives as soon as their objectives have positive effects on people.

1513. Positive principles help us achieve personal goals.

1514. Positive principles help us be more appreciated.

1515. The respect of the wife towards the husband is achieved through a positive behavior of her husband towards her and the other members of his family.

1516. Positive ideas should always be supported.

1517. Developing positive thinking leads to the creation of more positive ideas.

Peacemakers

1518. Responsibility helps us become peacemakers.

1519. Continuous self-motivation helps us become peacemakers.

1520. Optimism helps us become peacemakers.

1521. Continuously making ourselves efficient helps us become peacemakers.

1522. Confidence in ourselves helps us become peacemakers.

1523. Will helps us become peacemakers.

1524. Cherishing oneself helps us become peacemakers.

1525. Creativity helps us become peacemakers.

1526. The self efficient use of our time helps us become peacemakers.

1527. Continuous self perfection helps us become peacemakers.

1528. Acting efficiently helps us become peacemakers.

1529. Communication helps us become peacemakers.

1530. Wisdom helps us become peacemakers.

Perfecting

1531. Our own happiness can be achieved and maintained also through the contribution of the formation, development, maintenance and usage of continuous self perfecting behavior.

1532. Rather than lamenting that we do not have successes it is more useful to also form, develop, maintain and use of continuously self perfecting behavior.

1533. We can prevent some failures also through the contribution of the formation, development, maintenance and usage of continuous self perfecting behavior.

1534. Aspiring towards a more meaningful life can also be achieved through the formation, development, maintenance and usage of continuous self perfecting behavior.

1535. The radical transformation for the better of our life can be achieved also through the formation, development, maintenance and usage of continuous self perfecting behavior.

1536. Some mistakes can be prevented also through the contribution of the formation, development, maintenance and usage of continuous self-perfecting behavior.

1537. Our happiness depends a lot also on the formation, development, maintenance and usage of continuous self perfecting behavior.

1538. In order to prevent not achieving our personal goals, it is necessary to also form, develop, maintain and use our continuous self perfecting behavior.

1539. Hopes can be created also through the contribution of the formation, development, maintenance and usage of continuous self-perfecting behavior.

1540. We can overcome the difficulties that we must overcome also through the help of the formation, development, maintenance and usage of continuous self perfecting behavior.

1541. We can become stronger and we can not allow ourselves to be influenced by the world also through the contribution of the formation, development, maintenance and usage of continuous self perfecting behavior.

1542. Release from our self-imposed restrictions can be made also through the contribution of the formation, development, maintenance and usage of continuous self-perfecting behavior.

1543. Our resistance to changing for the better can be overcome also through the contribution of the formation, development, maintenance and usage of continuous self-perfecting behavior.

1544. We can contribute to the achievement of our greatest accomplishments also through the contribution of the formation, development, maintenance and usage of continuous self-perfecting behavior.

1545. In order to stand up once again for the first time or for the who knows what time, it is necessary to also form, develop, maintain and use a continuous self-perfecting behavior.

Performances

1546. The ability of achieving performances helps us achieve more successes.

1547. The ability of accomplishing records helps us achieve more performances.

1548. The desire to accomplish positive deeds helps us achieve more performances.

1549. The desire of achieving good deeds helps us achieve more performances.

1550. Persevering in ignoring the word NO helps us achieve more performances.

1551. The desire to achieve performances helps us achieve more successes.

1552. Never giving up helps us achieve more performances.

1553. Preventing accidents helps us achieve more performances.

1554. The power of continuous efficient organization helps us achieve more performances.

1555. The ability of achieving performances helps us achieve more favorable chances.

1556. Our positive attitude towards life helps us achieve more performances.

1557. Going on without stopping helps us achieve more performances.

1558. The ability of achieving performances helps us achieve more favorable situations.

1559. Not being concerned about what others might think of us helps us achieve more performances.

1560. The desire to achieve successes helps us achieve more performances.

1561. Learning from other people's mistakes helps us achieve more performances.

1562. The courage of not letting ourselves be stopped helps us achieve more performances.

1563. Rising from more failures helps us achieve more performances.

1564. The daily gathering of as much useful knowledge as possible helps us achieve more performances.

1565. Preventing worries helps us achieve more performances.

1566. Finding creative solutions that contribute to solving misunderstandings helps us achieve more performances.

1567. The accumulation of all data necessary for taking right decisions helps us achieve more performances.

1568. Preventing everything that harms young people helps us achieve more performances.

1569. The art of solving arguments helps us achieve more performances.

1570. The art of solving problems helps us achieve more performances.

1571. The desire to achieve performances helps us achieve more pleasant surprises.

1572. The power used to accomplish positive deeds helps us achieve more performances.

1573. Preventing the inefficient use of time helps us achieve more performances.

1574. Persevering in going against everybody's convictions helps us achieve more performances.

1575. The desire to achieve performances helps us achieve more favorable situations.

1576. The ability of achieving performances helps us achieve much good luck.

1577. The passion of accomplishing successes helps us achieve more performances.

1578. Permanent concentration on our personal objectives helps us achieve more performances.

1579. The ability to go against everybody's convictions helps us achieve more performances.

Perseverance

1580. In order to follow and transform our personal goals into reality, it is necessary to also form, develop, maintain and use our perseverance.

1581. Successful relationships can be achieved step by step and with perseverance.

1582. A happy life can be achieved also through perseverance.

1583. Perseverance often leads us to achieving successes.

1584. Obstacles that stop us from achieving our personal goals can be overcome by perseverance.

1585. Success in everything we do is a change also due to perseverance.

1586. A professional successful life is achieved only through perseverance.

1587. People on earth have sufficient resources to unite their huge forces, through solidarity, cooperation, co-development, perseverance, willpower, work, the Internet, the media, the mobile phone, etc., to install in record time in many places and situations normality instead of abnormalities. Start right now that you will always succeed for you are an invincible force, you can replace the abnormal with the normal in no matter what situations and places. Persevere until you succeed and if you need it, continually ask for help from other citizens of the planet that will join you to become incredibly many. Good luck. I am sure you will succeed.

1588. Fatigue can be prevented through the proper nutrition of the person concerned, through education, positive behavior, balanced life, intellectual exercises, perseverance, willpower, exercise, a value system that we believe in and that we respect, business dynamism, social relations, friends, mature love, a happy marriage, adequate rest when necessary, proper sleep, entertainment, etc..

1589. Good mood can be achieved if the person concerned has adequate nourishment, it can be achieved through education, intellectual work, perseverance, willpower, exercise, a value system that we believe in and that we respect, business dynamism, social relationships, friends, mature love and a happy marriage.

1590. Positive thinking can be achieved if you do not have it through the proper nutrition of the person concerned, through education, intellectual work, perseverance, experience, willingness, physical exercises, etc.

1591. A psychological balance can be maintain once achieved through the proper nutrition of the person concerned, through education, intellectual work, perseverance, experience, willingness, physical exercises, etc.

1592. Positive thinking can be maintained through a proper diet, education, intellectual exercise, perseverance, experience, will, physical exercises, etc.

1593. Psychical balance can be obtained through education, will, perseverance.

1594. Good humor can be maintained through a balanced life, a proper diet, education, intellectual exercises, psychical balance, perseverance, women, physical exercises, a value system in which we believe in and that we respect, positive activities, dynamism, social relations, friends, mature love, a happy marriage, etc.

1595. Those who seek favorable situations through perseverance and are better documented will find favorable situations.

1596. Perseverance is a key that has helped to achieve many successes.

Personality

1597. Permanently, continuously, day by day, for as long as we live it is necessary to have the personal goal to increasingly support education and self-education for children to achieve a harmonious personality.

1598. Harmonious global co-development thinking, the projects and programs of harmonious co-development assure the development of personality.

1599. Discrimination negatively affects the harmonious development of the personality of many children, very much, all over the world.

1600. States need to create material, financial, legal, time conditions required by parents to educate, advice, consult, raise their children properly, to develop their harmonious personality.

1601. Each parent is required to ensure continuously, day by day, for as long as they live, conditions, an environment and education necessary to increase the harmonious development of their children's personality.

1602. Constantly, every day, continuously, for as long as we live it is necessary to have as a personal goal the harmonious development of our personality.

1603. Each parent must deal with the growth and education of their children and as long as necessary to ensure the harmonious development of the personality of children.

1604. The states need and must build a sufficient number of kindergartens to ensure children's harmonious growth and education corresponding to their personality.

1605. Social thinking is necessary and required for the creation of a social system that ensures the harmonious development of the personality of each person.

1606. The harmonious development of the personality of children is a main factor of human progress and human society.

1607. It is needed to create financial and legal conditions, to give the time required by parents to educate, advise, consult, raise their children, to develop their harmonious personality.

1608. Each parent is required to ensure continuously, day by day, living conditions for the necessary growth and education of his children and for the harmonious development of their personality.

1609. The financing by the state of more positive, efficient initiatives, helpful to people and society should contribute a lot and would accelerate the development of their personality, their integration into society, from participating in the realization of many activities of society.

1610. An honest man has greater chances to harmoniously develop his personality.

Pessimism

1611. Pessimism can be removed and replaced with optimism also through the contribution of the formation, development, maintenance and usage of continuous self-controlling behavior.

1612. Pessimism can be removed and replaced with optimism also through the contribution of the formation, development, maintenance and usage of hardworking behavior.

1613. Pessimism can be removed and replaced with optimism also through the contribution of the formation, development, maintenance and usage of a behavior of being devoid of prejudices.

1614. Pessimism can be removed and replaced with optimism also through the contribution of the formation, development, maintenance and usage of brave behavior.

1615. Pessimism can be removed and replaced with optimism also through the contribution of the formation, development, maintenance and usage of demanding behavior.

1616. Pessimism can be removed and replaced with optimism also through the contribution of the formation, development, maintenance and usage of sociable behavior.

1617. Pessimism can be removed and replaced with optimism also through the contribution of the formation, development, maintenance and usage of calm behavior.

1618. Pessimism can be removed and replaced with optimism also through the contribution of the formation, development, maintenance and usage of sincere behavior.

1619. Pessimism can be removed and replaced with optimism also through the contribution of the formation, development, maintenance and usage of organized behavior.

1620. Pessimism can be removed and replaced with optimism also through the contribution of the formation, development, maintenance and usage of working behavior.

1621. Pessimism can be removed and replaced with optimism also through the contribution of the formation, development, maintenance and usage of trustworthy behavior.

1622. Pessimism can be removed and replaced with optimism also through the contribution of the formation, development, maintenance and usage of behavior of being receptive to new.

1623. Pessimism can be removed and replaced with optimism also through the contribution of the formation, development, maintenance and usage of persevering behavior.

1624. Pessimism can be removed and replaced with optimism also through the contribution of the formation, development, maintenance and usage of efficient behavior.

1625. Pessimism can be removed and replaced with optimism also through the contribution of the formation, development, maintenance and usage of diplomatic behavior.

Pleasure

1626. It gives you great pleasure to be in the company of a peaceful man.

1627. Mature love is due to the joining of the optimal intelligent rationality, accountability, realism and logic with pleasure, joy and mutual giving

1628. For those who have succeeded in life, who had one or more major successes, the effort they have made to pursue them without problems, to be consumed without having to make big efforts, they made such efforts on their own initiative, without them, someone would do them with great pleasure, without any stress, but it is considered that to succeed it is necessary to make those efforts, those actions. Although efforts, actions were very high, with huge consumption of mental and physical energy, more or less risks they felt of course, normal in order to achieve success, and what they proposed, and this is not to look at the facts not stressed, but on the contrary it has created a state of normality and even additional motivation and desire to do what they have proposed. These ones in contrast with others that the risky, unpredictable, great efforts chased, tried to solve, or attempted to carry out the enormous stress and had much inefficient behavior, but they always made them smarter, more effective, more operational, more powerful, more confident in their forces, in their success, in their future, etc

Polite

1629. The polite man must be appreciated.

1630. Polite people are also people with common sense.

1631. Polite people must be appreciated.

1632. Polite people must be respected.

1633. Polite people must be supported.

1634. Being polite makes us more pleasant in life.

1635. People who have had successes are most of the times also polite.

1636. Polite people also have good sense.

1637. Being polite is many times the key of successes.

1638. Being polite must always be promoted, supported, appreciated, respected and rewarded.

1639. Polite people easily and quickly make true friends.

1640. People who are polite are also kind.

1641. Polite people are respected, appreciated and esteemed.

1642. People who are polite achieve easier and faster social relations.

Precaution

1643. Precaution helps us achieve much good luck.

1644. Precaution helps us achieve more pleasant surprises.

1645. Precaution helps us achieve more successes.

1646. Precaution helps us achieve more favorable situations.

1647. Precaution helps us achieve more performances

1648. People, it's good to find our right half to use all possibilities, but at each party to take all precautionary measures to prevent unpleasant surprises. You will succeed. Persevere and use the Internet. Good luck.

Possibilities

1649. An enterprising spirit increases our possibilities of achieving more social relations.

1650. The sense of achievement and quality in everything we do creates much more possibilities to participate in achieving efficient global co operations.

1651. A positive enterprising spirit creates greater possibilities to create a more beautiful life.

1652. Those who have high objectives in life have great possibilities to participate in very efficient co operations.

1653. The ability of rapids perception increases our possibilities of preventing many unpleasant surprises.

1654. Combining our knowledge increases our possibilities to achieve more and greater successes.

1655. Humanist global thinking creates great possibilities of accelerating the resolution of many human problems in all the countries of the world.

1656. An intelligent man has much more possibilities to achieve efficient co operations.

1657. The ability of rapid perception increases our possibilities of achieving outstanding performances.

1658. Combining our knowledge increases our possibilities of achieving more and greater successes.

1659. A strategic vision increases our possibilities of achieving more and greater successes.

1660. A man with imagination has great possibilities of contributing to the formation and development of global thinking.

1661. Responsible people have much more possibilities of contributing to achieving a positive global future.

1662. Orientation towards a goal increases our possibilities of achieving a successful marriage.

1663. The ability to take rapid decisions increases our possibilities of achieving our personal goals a lot faster.

1664. Increasing the strengths of our mind arguments are possibilities of achieving more and greater successes a lot.

1665. Increasing the strength of our mind augments our possibilities of achieving more efficient co-developments a lot.

1666. Combining our knowledge increases our possibilities of achieving our personal goals.

1667. Those who build their life on rational conscious bases have great possibilities of success.

1668. A common man that approaches problems simultaneously from different points of view has more chances and possibilities of becoming even more efficient.

1669. Reasonable men have more possibilities of maintaining a happy marriage.

1670. People who are resistant to stress have the chances and possibilities of becoming more credible.

1671. Studying day by day, continuously, for as long as we live, the life of people around us, of those who have successes, we have great possibilities of finding many efficient positive behaviors that can help us a lot in achieving our personal goals.

1672. Permanent self education used in solving personal problems increases our trust in ourselves and in our possibilities.

1673. Those with the ability to dissociate emotions from their responsibilities have greater chances and possibilities to maintain true friendships.

1674. The orientation toward a goal increases our possibilities to achieve outstanding performances.

1675. For people in the world's states there are much more chances and possibilities to obtain a more beautiful life with the help of technology.

1676. Presently, mankind has enormously many possibilities of development in the favor and towards the good and happiness of mankind.

Potential

1677. Imagination can be developed with low psychical efforts but with potentially great effects.

1678. Positive ideas prevent many potential conflicts.

1679. Those who know that discipline is the key of dreams have the potential to achieve their own happiness.

1680. Positive thinking helps us prevent many potential unpleasant surprises.

1681. A creative man has an even greater potential to become more efficient.

1682. Those who have had better social and economic all conditions during their evolution have a greater potential to maintain the desired true friendships.

1683. Most of those involved in more projects have the potential to achieve efficient co-developments.

1684. Those who control circumstances have a greater potential to achieve true friendships.

1685. Those who discover unique ways to work efficiently for a better life have a greater potential to achieve outstanding performances.

1686. The need to succeed makes a man avoid much more potential mistakes.

1687. A man who acts continuously, day by day, to be even more efficient has more and greater chances and a higher potential to achieve greater performances.

1688. A man satisfied with his own way of behaving socially has great chances and a high potential to achieve more and greater successes.

1689. A man who approaches and is used to approach problems simultaneously from different points of view has great chances and a high potential to achieve his personal goals.

1690. Ambitious people have a greater potential to become even more efficient.

1691. Ambitious men have a greater potential to achieve their personal goals.

1692. Those who voluntarily assume certain risks only when they have an increased chance of reaching their objective have a great potential to achieve more efficient co operations.

1693. Those who possess the ability to dissociate emotions from their responsibilities have a greater potential to succeed in life.

1694. Those who build their life on rationally conscious bases have a greater potential to achieve personal goals.

1695. A man oriented towards the outside world has more and greater chances and a greater potential to develop efficiently.

1696. A realistic man in interpersonal relations has much more and greater chances and a higher potential to achieve more true friendships.

1697. A man who acts day by day, continuously to become even more efficient has much more and greater chances and a higher potential to meet even more favorable situations.

1698. A man open towards new ideas has much more chances and a greater potential to achieve a true mature love.

1699. A man who approaches and is used to approach problems simultaneously from different points of view has the chances and a great potential to achieve a more beautiful life.

1700. A man willing to try new ways has the chances and the great potential to achieve efficient co-developments.

Practical

1701. A great capacity of having an even more energetic life helps us become practical.

1702. A great capacity of using qualities helps us maintain our way of being practical.

1703. A great capacity of being creative in order to solve great problems helps us become practical.

1704. A great capacity of more efficiently using time helps us become more practical.

1705. A great capacity of assuming the necessary risks for achieving great successes helps us maintain our way of being practical.

1706. A great capacity of assuming the necessary risks for achieving personal goals helps us maintain our way of being practical.

1707. A great capacity of being creative in order to solve great problems helps us maintain our way of being practical.

1708. A great capacity of being honest with oneself helps us maintain our way of being practical.

1709. A great capacity of remaining involved in the same area with even greater objectives helps us maintain our way of being practical.

1710. A great capacity of dealing with pressures no matter how great they are helps us become practical.

1711. Adaptation helps us become more practical.

1712. A great capacity of establishing high personal goals helps us become practical.

1713. A great capacity of analyzing a situation logically helps us become more practical.

1714. A great capacity of continuous self perfection helps us become more practical.

1715. A great capacity of having one's own principles and not letting one be influenced by the negative opinions of others helps us maintain our way of being practical.

1716. Continuous self perfection helps us become practical.

1717. A great capacity of gathering our energies helps us maintain our way of being practical.

1718. A great capacity of having an even more energetic life helps us maintain our way of being practical.

1719. The dream to the grand helps us maintain our way of being practical.

1720. Inter-human communication sometimes helps us become more practical.

1721. Will helps us be practical.

1722. Wisdom helps us become more practical.

1723. The desire to make others happy can be achieved through the contribution of the formation, and development, maintenance and usage of practical ideas.

1724. A man who has practical values most of the times knows how to efficiently and practically manage his time.

1725. A man who has practical values usually knows how to harmoniously develop his personality.

1726. A man with practical values manages to accomplish efficient co operations.

1727. A man who has practical values has more and greater chances of achieving more and greater successes.

1728. Taken from anyone, any practical ideas help you in life to achieve your personal goals.

1729. A man with practical values succeeds in earning his living for life.

Preventive

1730. A great capacity of dealing with pressures, no matter how great they are, helps us become more preventive.

1731. A great capacity of using each injustice received in order to achieve successes helps us become more preventive.

1732. A great capacity of thinking largely helps us become more preventive.

1733. A great capacity of being understanding with people helps us become more preventive.

1734. A great capacity of learning how to achieve personal goals helps us become more preventive.

1735. A great capacity of remaining involved in the same area with even greater objectives helps us become more preventive.

1736. A great capacity of accomplishing strategies of applying thinking on a big scale helps us become more preventive.

1737. A great capacity of using each personal mistake to achieve successes helps us become more preventive.

1738. A great capacity of assuming the necessary risks for achieving personal goals helps us become more preventive.

1739. A great capacity of analyzing a situation logically helps us become more preventive.

1740. A great capacity of more efficiently using financial means helps us become more preventive.

1741. A great capacity of continuously enhancing performances helps us become more preventive.

1742. A great capacity of increasing self confidence helps us become more preventive.

1743. A great capacity of establishing high personal goals helps us become more preventive.

1744. A great capacity of achieving what was proposed helps us become more preventive.

1745. A great capacity of assuming the necessary risks for success helps us become more preventive.

1746. A great capacity of using available knowledge helps us become more preventive.

1747. A great capacity of having one's own principles and not letting one be influenced by the negative opinions of others helps us become more preventive.

1748. A great capacity of using each failure to achieve successes helps us become more preventive.

1749. Preventive thinking must be maintained.

1750. Using preventive thinking requires many exchanges of information.

1751. Preventive thinking contributes a lot in achieving efficient co operations.

1752. Using preventive thinking helps in the achievement of some positive social relations.

1753. Using preventive thinking contributes to the development of global thinking.

1754. Using preventive thinking helps us achieve our own happiness.

1755. Preventive thinking must be promoted.

1756. Using preventive thinking helps us a lot in life.

1757. Using preventive thinking increases our participation in achieving the greater good.

Pride

1758. The self-control of our behaviors helps us a lot to prevent pride.

1759. Pride removes the proud one from the others.

1760. Children are suffering very high mental trauma when parents divorce. Dear parents, if you have children, before the divorce, look to find solutions to prevent the divorce and to achieve a happy marriage for both you and your children. To be sure you have the qualities required and can perform a real, happy marriage, if both of you cooperate sincerely, if you are both more tolerant with each other, if you make all the compromises necessary, if you do not worry about all kinds of complexes, if you want to understand the other, if you lose pride to nonsense, if you do what is necessary for both spouses and children to be happy and there is no need to do something the other does not desire, but what the situation requires to have a happy marriage. Trust in yourselves, you do not play with your marriage, your children, with your happiness because you have the qualities necessary to have a happy marriage and happy children and to surpass all the difficulties that appear.

1761. Pride must not be found between those who cooperate.

Qualities

1762. Each of us surely has a higher or lower number of qualities. It is for our own good and for our happiness to discover them and then to use them as much as we can in order to make us happy.

1763. Each of us surely has a higher or lower number of qualities. It is for our own good and for our happiness to discover them and then to use them as much as we can in order to make us happy.

1764. Each of us has a bigger or smaller number of qualities.

1765. It is never too late to self-develop certain qualities.

1766. It is necessary at all times to develop our human qualities.

1767. Those that have more qualities have more opportunities to make themselves happy.

1768. Our qualities make a lot of us very happy.

1769. Human qualities contribute the most to human success.

1770. Young people of the world's states, unfortunately, do not use their capacities and qualities, skills, abilities, attitudes, knowledge, and the enormous energy that they have, their enthusiasm and optimism, which are positive things, the desire of affirmation and of making achievements in order to participate in the activity of communal, municipal, departmental, regional councils of counties, of parliaments, of governments, etc..

1771. Human qualities contribute the most to human successes.

1772. Human qualities make a lot of people happy.

1773. Persons with many qualities are respected.

1774. Persons with many qualities are valued.

1775. Persons with many qualities are more likely to achieve more successes than those who have fewer skills.

1776. Persons with many qualities have very big chances to achieve successes.

1777. A man with qualities is appreciated.

1778. The more qualities we have, the more and greater opportunities we have to achieve more successes.

1779. The fact that we do not have certain assets, accomplishments, etc. during certain periods of our life must not fret, consume, frustrate, make us unhappy, but it is necessary to enjoy what we have, what we have achieved, the projects that we have to achieve, the qualities, the skills that we have, etc.

1780. I esteem women very much, appreciate and respect them very much for what they are, for the special qualities that they have.

1781. It is essential that much more women set as goals the prevention of divorce, of unhappy marriages and that they work to achieve them, because fortunately they will most certainly succeed because many have the qualities and capabilities required to do this.

1782. By developing their inner beauty, the qualities, skills, abilities and feelings that make them happy, women can create more joy and satisfactions.

1783. Knowing yourself is very necessary and very useful to us in order to achieve a happy marriage, to maintain it, to make friends and to maintain them, to use cover our qualities and flaws, etc.

1784. Men need to appreciate, respect all the qualities of women no matter what the situation is, even in this situation when these have more qualities than them.

1785. The husband who has a wife with more qualities than he does needs to be proud of her, to respect her, appreciate and support her, help her use her qualities for her sake, their children's sake and her husband's sake.

1786. The life of each of us is influenced by us once, that is the by our internal factors, which are very large in number, among which we can remember: 1) our health, 2) our values, 3) our objectives, 4) our qualities 5) our thinking, 6) if we think long term or short-term, or joined, completed, 7) our ability, 8) our gender, 9) our age, etc.

Respect

1787. They deserve to be appreciated, honored, respected and rewarded, all those journalists who do not act by order to unjustly hit some people, or groups of people.

1788. The correct behavior of a man towards his wife and other members of his family makes that man be very respected by his wife and members of his family.

1789. If we respect principles we will be more respected.

1790. Respecting principles helps us maintain true friendships.

1791. Prominent people must be respected for the good they do for mankind.

1792. Unfortunately in most of the world states there are still illegal court orders that do not respect human rights.

1793. Our life has been given to us so that we live it, but not in any way, mocking it, at chance, but thoughtly, economisingly, planningly, with good sense, with hopes, with positive thoughts and actions, with humanities, with love, with dedication only with what does us and others good. Good luck.

1794. You will succeed if you respect what there is to be respected, what you very well know and what must be respected. Good luck again.

1795. Fatigue can be prevented through the proper nutrition of the person concerned, through education, positive behavior, balanced life, intellectual exercises, perseverance, willpower, exercise, a value system that we believe in and that we respect, business dynamism, social relations, friends, mature love, a happy marriage, adequate rest when necessary, proper sleep, entertainment, etc..

1796. Self control must always be promoted, sustained, appreciated, respected and rewarded.

1797. Work must always be promoted, sustained, appreciated, respected and rewarded.

1798. Independence must always be promoted, appreciated, respected and rewarded.

1799. The sense of responsibility needs to be appreciated, promoted, supported and respected.

1800. Men must respect women who earn more than they do.

1801. People need and must act to sue all the elected and dignitaries, public clerks who do not respect their rights, who created damages.

1802. Honor must be promoted, supported, appreciated, respected and rewarded.

React

1803. We must know why we react like this.

1804. The ability to react with understanding help us make more friends.

1805. The ability to react to understanding helps us achieve a happy marriage.

Receptive

1806. Hopes can be created also through the contribution of the formation, development, maintenance and usage of receptive to new behavior.

1807. In order to stand up once again for the first time or for the who knows what time, it is necessary to also form, develop, maintain and use receptive to new behavior.

1808. Pessimism can be removed and replaced with optimism also through the contribution of the formation, development, maintenance and usage of behavior of being receptive to new.

Reciprocal

1809. Man's most beautiful ideal is that of achieving a true reciprocal love.

1810. Reciprocal love makes us more optimistic.

1811. True reciprocal love makes the lovers desire to merge, unite with each other, they achieve each other reciprocally through total giving, including through sex until total exhaustion.

Resistance

1812. Our resistance to changing for the better can be overcome also through the contribution of the formation, development, maintenance and usage of a behavior of being in love with life.

1813. Our resistance to changing for the better can be overcome also through the contribution of the formation, development, maintenance and usage of continuous self-effecting behavior.

1814. Our resistance to changing for the better can be overcome also through the contribution of the formation, development, maintenance and usage of creative behavior.

1815. Our resistance to changing for the better can be overcome also through the contribution of the formation, development, maintenance and usage of sturdy behavior.

1816. Our resistance to changing for the better can be overcome also through the contribution of the formation, development, maintenance and usage of trained behavior.

1817. Our resistance to changing for the better can be overcome also through the contribution of the formation, development, maintenance and usage of stimulating behavior.

1818. Resistance to change for the better can be defeated and overcome also through the formation, development, maintenance and usage of the ability to be brave.

1819. Those who have a greater resistance to stress have more and greater chances to achieve efficient co operations.

1820. Those who have resistance to stress have a greater ability to contribute to achieving the greater good.

1821. Those with a greater resistance to stress have more chances to succeed in life.

1822. Those with a greater resistance to stress must be appreciated.

1823. Those with a greater resistance to stress have more and greater chances to achieve their personal goals.

1824. Those with a greater resistance to stress have more and greater chances to achieve more and greater successes.

1825. Those with a greater resistance to stress have higher chances to maintain efficient co operations.

1826. Those with a greater resistance to stress have higher chances to achieve themselves.

1827. Very sociable people have a higher resistance to stress.

1828. Our resistance to changing for the better can be overcome also through the contribution of the formation, development, maintenance and usage of diplomatic behavior.

1829. Our resistance to changing for the better can be overcome also through the contribution of the formation, development, maintenance and usage of tolerant behavior.

Responsibilities

1830. We can prevent the formation of new problems also through the formation, development, maintenance and usage of the ability to cope with the responsibilities.

1831. Abilities can be formed, developed, maintained and used also through the contribution of the formation, development, maintenance and usage of the ability to face responsibilities.

1832. Obstacles that stop us from achieving our personal goals can be overcome also through the contribution of the formation, development, maintenance and usage of the ability to dissociate emotions from responsibilities.

1833. Our abilities can be formed, developed, maintained and used also through the contribution of the formation, development, maintenance and usage of the ability to cope with responsibilities.

1834. Those who possess the capacity to dissociate emotions from their responsibilities have a greater potential to contribute in achieving a positive global future.

1835. Constructive thinking makes us have zero adversities towards responsibilities.

1836. Those with the ability to dissociate emotions from their responsibilities have greater chances and possibilities to maintain true friendships.

1837. Those who have the ability to dissociate emotions from their responsibilities have higher chances and a greater potential to achieve more and higher successes.

Rigorous

1838. Our resistance to changing for the better can be overcome also through the contribution of the formation, development, maintenance and usage of rigorous behavior.

1839. Continuous self-motivation helps us become rigorous.

1840. We can overcome the difficulties that we must overcome also through the help of the formation, development, maintenance and usage of rigorous behavior.

1841. The necessary qualities in achieving personal goals can be formed, developed, maintained and used also through the contribution of the formation, development, maintenance and usage of rigorous behavior.

1842. In achieving our successes a contribution is also brought by the formation, development, maintenance and usage of rigorous behavior.

1843. We can form, develop and maintain the state of being ourselves also through the contribution of the formation, development, maintenance and usage of a rigorous behavior.

1844. Our own happiness can be achieved and maintained also through the contribution of the formation, development, maintenance and usage of rigorous behavior.

1845. We can prevent the falling apart of a happy marriage also through the contribution of the formation, development, maintenance and usage of rigorous behavior.

1846. Self-imposed discipline helps us become rigorous.

1847. Our happiness depends a lot also on the formation, development, maintenance and usage of rigorous behavior.

1848. The limits of achievement imposed by ourselves in our mind at a given moment can be overcome or eliminated also through the contribution of the formation, development, maintenance and usage of rigorous behavior.

1849. The obstacles that prevent us from achieving our personal goals can be surpassed also through the contribution of the formation, development, maintenance and usage of rigorous behavior.

1850. Obtaining more and greater successes can be achieved also through the contribution of the formation, development, maintenance, usage of a rigorous behavior.

1851. The solutions to the problems we have or that we want to solve can be found also through the contribution of the formation, development, maintenance and usage of rigorous behavior.

1852. In order to rise up once again for the first time for the who knows what time it is necessary to also form, develop, maintain and use rigorous behavior.

Responsibility

1853. Responsibility helps us become trained.

1854. Responsibility helps us become firm.

1855. Responsibility helps us become peacemakers.

Responsible

1856. Obtaining more and greater successes can be achieved also through the contribution of the formation, development, maintenance, usage of a responsible behavior.

1857. We can form, develop and maintain the state of being ourselves also through the contribution of the formation, development, maintenance and usage of a responsible behavior.

1858. In order to escape poverty it is necessary to also form, develop, maintain and use responsible behavior.

Routine

1859. Routine is very necessary and useful in behavior, etc. In actions for a certain period of time. After a certain period of time, at a certain time it is necessary to get rid of a certain routine, a certain behavior, a way of thinking, a certain kind of action, etc.. And replace it with another behavior more efficiently, more operational, more tactful, more thoughtful, etc.. In order to progress in achieving what we proposed, our personal objectives. When we need to get rid, to escape a certain routine it is necessary to get rid of it immediately, without doubts, delay, fears, etc. And to act in the new action, new behavior more effectively, without any delay. People who have the ability to leave a certain routine immediately when they need to, progress much faster in life, carry out much faster and more efficient personal goals, performe in live many more bigger or smaller successes than those who do not get rid of a particular or specific routine when necessary. Routine, when we get rid of it when necessary is a big negative factor of progress, it creates many failures, misfortunes, difficulties in achieving personal goals in life, it creates misunderstandings in families and may even lead to divorce, misunderstandings and even conflicts between large generations etc.. The routine of a normal fact, when we can not get rid of it, and it is necessary to get rid of it, it may actually become a very harmful fact for our new family, for the people around, for society, for younger generations and for the future, it may sometimes have many negative effects, very large and very diverse ones. For these reasons it is necessary to continuously develop our ability to get rid of routine when needed immediately.

Self- development

1860. Spiritual self-development helps and contributes greatly to self-progress in other actions and activities.

1861. By spiritual self-development, we can surely achieve a better life.

1862. Spiritual self-development, that of each of us contributes to building a better world.

1863. Mental self-development is necessary and required to be achieved, continuously, day by day, for as long as we live.

1864. Mental self-development, continuously, day by day, helps us contribute greatly to achieving other objectives.

1865. Phisical self-development and maintenance, continually, day by day, is necessary to be achieved.

1866. As a personal goal, for as long as we live, it is necessary and required to have both physical self-development and maintenance, continually, day by day.

1867. By maintaining physical self-development, continuously, day by day, our personal goals, helps us live to achieve other personal goals.

1868. Spiritual self-development is one of the personal self-developments that we can do ourselves.

1869. Spiritual self-development helps us very much to develop spiritually. Spiritual self-development should be one of the main objectives of our personal life as it has many positive effects on us and on the others and for society.Having as a personal objective personal self-development and if we achieve it for as long as we live, we will be able to progress and develop incredibly much spiritually and we automatically create opportunities to achieve bigger or smaller successes in life.

1870. Spiritual self-development is necessary, it is useful and it should become mandatory for each person as a personal goal due to the importance, necessity, utility, the requirement for spiritual development of each person of this planet, of countries and of all mankind. Spiritual self-development is a major highly efficient form of the development of our spiritual life.

1871. To increase the number of people who will set as a personal goal the spiritual self-development and who will create greater opportunities for spiritual self-development to be done by as many people as possible who aimed for self-development as a personal goal, it is necessary to continuously create and develop the science of personal development which encompasses the spiritual and scientific personal self-development. Until we create and develop the science of spiritual development it is necessary to develop the science of spiritual self-development because so many people from many countries are more active and effective than the countries in which they live and thus they can be models for other people with positive models of personal self-development and so they can help them create and develop, achieve their personal objectives.

1872. Unfortunately, at present there is no science of spiritual development, no science of spiritual self-development, and there are not many people who have set the objective of personal spiritual self-development, although spiritual self-development is extremely necessary and very useful to each person and society as a whole. Because of these shortcomings and large utilities for its individual and society, it is very useful and very necessary that as many people as possible establish as a goal the personal self-development and have personal dedication to this goal for as long as they live to achieve themselves continuously and not wait until society or certain private or state institutions will create the science of spiritual development and the science of spiritual self-development.

1873. Spiritual self-development will help us greatly in spiritual development that can be accelerated if we continually study the issues that can help us grow spiritually, issues that we find stored in books, publications, television, on the Internet, in the life experience of people who have values and ethics and have achieved many and great successes thanks to the development of their spirituality and ethic. The longer we self-develop spiritually the more opportunities we have to achieve more and greater successes that are made by spiritual self-development.

1874. Spiritual self-development unfortunately although it is very necessary and useful both to each man and society, humanity, it does not exist as a personal goal to most people in the world.

1875. Mental self-development helps mostly to our mental development. Mental self-development is necessary and required to become a personal goal for as long as we live for every earthling.

1876. Spiritual self-development helps mostly the spiritual development of each human being.

1877. Spiritual self-development is necessary and required due to its importance for each human to become a personal goal for as long as we live.

1878. Mental self-development enormously increases our chances and creates much more to get more and greater successes for as long as we live.

1879. Mental self-development enormously increases our possibilities to set more and greater personal life targets and achieve them.

1880. Mental self-development enormously increases our efficiency and productivity of our thinking for as long as we live, on a continuous basis.

1881. Mental self-development enormously increases with much efficiency, productivity our actions with tremendous positive effects so that we can cooperate with others and with society.

1882. Mental self-development increases our efficiency with which we take personal decisions for others and for society, it greatly enhances the quality of the decisions we make, it greatly enhances the quality of our personal actions and those that co-ordinate them.

1883. Mental self-development is of enormous help in preventing a lot of failures, sorrows, mistakes, illnesses, accidents, conflicts, arguments, divorces, negative actions, inefficiencies, etc.

1884. Mental self-development continues for as long as we live and it helps us infinitely in achieving much more grater successes, performances, records, good deeds, positive actions, collaborations, ideas, books or movies creations, etc.

1885. The more time we dedicate daily to our mental self-development, the more chances we have to develop our mind more and more, and doing this, in its turn, shall help us even more in achieving a larger amount of personal objectives, and in a shorter and more productive time.

1886. Continuous mental self-development greatly increases our possibilities of achieving many successes.

1887. Continuous mental self-development greatly increases our opportunities to resolve personal goals.

1888. Continuous mental self-development increases our opportunities to succeed and to educate children to be raised much better.

1889. Spiritual self-development done continuously, day by day, for as long as we live continually increases our chances to achieve personal goals.

Sincere

1890. Optimism helps us become sincere.

1891. Hope helps us become sincere.

1892. Confidence in ourselves helps us become sincere.

1893. The force of our ideas can be augmented also through the contribution of the formation, development, maintenance and usage of sincere behavior.

1894. We can prevent some failures also through the contribution of the formation, development, maintenance and usage of sincere behavior.

1895. We can form, develop and maintain the state of being ourselves also through the contribution of the formation, development, maintenance and usage of a sincere behavior.

Sincerely

1896. Children are suffering very high mental trauma when parents divorce. Dear parents, if you have children, before the divorce, look to find solutions to prevent the divorce and to achieve a happy marriage for both you and your children. To be sure you have the qualities required and can perform a real, happy marriage, if both of you cooperate sincerely, if you are both more tolerant with each other, if you make all the compromises necessary, if you do not worry about all kinds of complexes, if you want to understand the other, if you lose pride to nonsense, if you do what is necessary for both spouses and children to be happy and there is no need to do something the other does not desire, but what the situation requires to have a happy marriage. Trust in yourselves, you do not play with your marriage, your children, with your happiness because you have the qualities necessary to have a happy marriage and happy children and to surpass all the difficulties that appear.

Sincerity

1897. Sincerity contributes greatly to the achievement of mature love.

1898. Sincerity is a quality that maintains a real marriage.

1899. Sincerity is a quality that contributes greatly to maintaining mature love.

Success

1900. Confidence in the success of what we do helps us achieve more favorable chances.

1901. A great capacity of assuming the necessary risks for success helps us maintain our happiness.

1902. A great capacity of assuming the necessary risks for success helps us maintain our way of being loving.

Successes

1903. Preventing conflicts helps us achieve more successes.

1904. Finding creative solutions that contribute to solving conflicts helps us achieve more successes.

1905. Using our passion helps us achieve more successes.

Selfishness

1906. Selfishness harms us a lot.

1907. Selfishness is one of the behaviors that stop the achievement of efficient co operations.

1908. Selfishness is one of the behaviors that stop the solving of many human problems.

Spontaneous

1909. People who have success voluntarily assume only when they have spontaneous successes the achievement of the goal.

1910. In order to follow and transform our personal goals into reality, it is necessary to also form, develop, maintain and use our spontaneous behavior.

1911. Hope helps us become spontaneous.

1912. The force of our ideas can be augmented also through the contribution of the formation, development, maintenance and usage of spontaneous behavior.

1913. Stress can be prevented also through the formation, development, maintenance and usage of spontaneous behavior.

1914. We can form, develop and maintain the state of being ourselves also through the contribution of the formation, development, maintenance and usage of a spontaneous behavior.

1915. In order to escape poverty it is necessary to also form, develop, maintain and use spontaneous behavior.

1916. Communication helps us become spontaneous.

1917. Creativity helps us become spontaneous.

1918. Will helps us become spontaneous.

1919. Obtaining more and greater successes can be achieved also through the contribution of the formation, development, maintenance, usage of a spontaneous behavior.

1920. The solutions to the problems we have or that we want to solve can be found also through the contribution of the formation, development, maintenance and usage of spontaneous behavior.

1921. Cherishing oneself helps us become spontaneous.

1922. Aspiring towards a more meaningful life can also be achieved through the formation, development, maintenance and usage of spontaneous behavior.

1923. Positive experience can be achieved also through the contribution of the formation, development, maintenance and usage of spontaneous behavior.

1924. Optimism helps us become spontaneous.

1925. Self-imposed discipline helps us become spontaneous.

1926. Our own happiness can be achieved and maintained also through the contribution of the formation, development, maintenance and usage of spontaneous behavior.

1927. In order to prevent not achieving our personal goals, it is necessary to also form, develop, maintain and use our spontaneous behavior.

1928. We can overcome the difficulties that we must overcome also through the help of the formation, development, maintenance and usage of spontaneous behavior.

1929. Rather than lamenting that we do not have successes it is more useful to also form, develop, maintain and use spontaneous behavior.

1930. In order to rise up once again for the first time for the who knows what time it is necessary to also form, develop, maintain and use spontaneous behavior.

1931. Continuous self-motivation helps us become spontaneous.

1932. Continuous self perfection helps us become spontaneous.

1933. We can prevent some failures also through the contribution of the formation, development, maintenance and usage of spontaneous behavior.

1934. Pessimism can be removed and replaced with optimism also through the contribution of the formation, development, maintenance and usage of spontaneous behavior.

1935. We can become stronger and we can not allow ourselves to be influenced by the world also through the contribution of the formation, development, maintenance and usage of spontaneous behavior.

1936. The necessary qualities in achieving personal goals can be formed, developed, maintained and used also through the contribution of the formation, development, maintenance and usage of spontaneous behavior.

1937. Wisdom helps us become spontaneous.

1938. Our resistance to changing for the better can be overcome also through the contribution of the formation, development, maintenance and usage of spontaneous behavior.

1939. Confidence in ourselves helps us become spontaneous.

1940. Our future can be projected and achieved also through the contribution of the formation, development, maintenance and usage of spontaneous behavior.

1941. We can contribute to the achievement of our greatest accomplishments also through the contribution of the formation, development, maintenance and usage of spontaneous behavior.

1942. Continuously making ourselves efficient helps us become spontaneous.

1943. Acting efficiently helps us become spontaneous.

1944. Continuous self-control helps us become spontaneous.

1945. Responsibility helps us become spontaneous.

1946. Release from our self-imposed restrictions can be made also through the contribution of the formation, development, maintenance and usage of spontaneous behavior.

1947. In achieving our successes a contribution is also brought by the formation, development, maintenance and usage of spontaneous behavior.

1948. Problems cannot be solved by the ideas that created them but also through the contribution of the formation, development, maintenance and usage of spontaneous behavior.

1949. Some mistakes can be prevented also through the contribution of the formation, development, maintenance and usage of spontaneous behavior.

1950. The self efficient use of our time helps us become spontaneous.

Sociable

1951. Sociable people must sometimes make sacrifices in their work place.

1952. Most of those who have not succeeded in building a happy marriage up to a certain date, in order to succeed they need to perfect and develop the ability of formation, development and maintenance of a sociable nature.

1953. Those who have high goals in life mostly have a sociable nature.

1954. A sociable man often makes exchanges of information.

1955. Very sociable and open people have much more chances to achieve true friendships.

1956. Very sociable people must be appreciated.

1957. Very sociable people are very willing to participate in achieving efficient global co operations

1958. Very sociable people have greater chances to achieve their own happiness.

1959. Very sociable people have more chances to succeed in life.

1960. A very sociable man is very much respected.

1961. A very sociable and open people have much more chances to achieve efficient co operations.

1962. A sociable man more quickly and easily achieves efficient co operations.

Sorrows

1963. Mental self-development is of enormous help in preventing a lot of failures, sorrows, mistakes, illnesses, accidents, conflicts, arguments, divorces, negative actions, inefficiencies, etc.

1964. Our objectivity helps us prevent many sorrows.

1965. We can prevent sorrows through a positive thinking.

1966. Frequent sorrows are bad for our health.

1967. Sorrows sometimes complicate problems even more.

1968. Sorrows that are often do us much harm.

Stress

1969. Stress can be prevented also through the formation, development, maintenance and usage of diplomatic behavior.

1970. Stress can be prevented also through the formation, development, maintenance and usage of sturdy behavior.

1971. Stress can be prevented also through the formation, development, maintenance and usage of efficient behavior.

1972. Stress can be prevented also through the formation, development, maintenance and usage of persevering behavior.

1973. People who are resistant to stress have more chances to contribute to increasing the efficiency of the group they are in.

1974. Sociable individuals are more resistant to stress than lonely people.

1975. Those who are not stressed are less wrong.

1976. Those who are not stressed have fewer failures.

1977. Laugh prevents stress.

1978. Laugh helps us reduce stress.

1979. Good humor prevents stress.

1980. Cheerfulness prevents stress.

1981. Continuous, long, sometimes much stress leads some people into depression.

1982. Cheerfulness helps us get rid of stress.

Successful

1983. Patience has contributed a lot to achieving very successful marriages.

1984. People who are most able in the majority of situations to apply their ideas have been more successful in life.

1985. Successful people have a great ability to cope with mental stress.

1986. Continuously making ourselves efficient helps us achieve more successes.

1987. Obtaining more and greater successes can be achieved also through the contribution of the formation, development, maintenance, usage of a firm behavior.

1988. Rather than lamenting that we do not have successes it is more useful to also form, develop, maintain and use decisive behavior.

1989. Obtaining more and greater successes can be achieved also through the contribution of the formation, development, maintenance, usage of a systematic behavior.

1990. Rather than lamenting that we do not have successes it is more useful to also form, develop, maintain and use expansive behavior.

1991. Rather than lamenting that we do not have successes it is more useful to also form, develop, maintain and use demanding behavior.

1992. A great capacity of using each personal mistake to achieve successes helps us become more pleasant.

Strength

1993. Optimism increases our strength.

1994. The common values of friends increase their confidence in the strength of their friendship.

1995. Positive human solidarity increases our human strength.

1996. Developing our thinking can be achieved and strengthened and we cannot read ourselves be influenced by the world also through the contribution of the formation, development, maintenance and usage of efficient actions.

1997. Increasing the strengths of our mind arguments are possibilities of achieving more and greater successes a lot.

1998. Developing our thinking can be achieved and strengthened and we cannot let ourselves be influenced by the world also through the contribution of the formation, development, maintenance and usage of some efficient actions.

1999. Women need to unite, to stay together and to cooperate in order to create a better world, because they have the abilities, the aptitudes, the qualities and the strength necessary to succeed.

2000. The strength of the mind is always more powerful than physical strength.

2001. Each of us must have the strength and willpower to prevent negative feelings, to maintain and develop happiness because they are extremely harmful for us and for others.

True

2002. Discovering true passion helps us achieve more favorable situations.

2003. The faithfulness of collaborators helps us achieve more true friendships.

2004. A man who is ready at any time to help someone has more chances to achieve a true love.

Truely

2005. When you are truely in love your whole body feels love.

2006. You really know what it means to love only when you have loved or when you truely love.

Truly

2007. The one who truly loves and is loved by the very person whom he loves, feels really alive.

2008. You really understand what love is about only when you have loved or when you truly love and have been truly loved or are truly loved by the person you love or have loved.

2009. Those who truly love people have much more chances to maintain a happy marriage.

Trust

2010. Our own happiness can be achieved and maintained also through the contribution of the formation, development, maintenance and usage of trustworthy behavior.

2011. Pessimism can be removed and replaced with optimism also through the contribution of the formation, development, maintenance and usage of trustworthy behavior.

2012. Release from our self-imposed restrictions can be made also through the contribution of the formation, development, maintenance and usage of trust-worthy behavior.

2013. The limits of achievement imposed by ourselves in our mind at a given moment can be overcome or eliminated also through the contribution of the formation, development, maintenance and usage of trust-worthy behavior.

2014. In order to prevent failures it is necessary to also form, develop, maintain and use trustworthy behavior.

2015. Obtaining more and greater successes can be achieved also through the contribution of the formation, development, maintenance, usage of a trustworthy behavior.

2016. We can contribute to the achievement of our greatest accomplishments also through the contribution of the formation, development, maintenance and usage of trustworthy behavior.

2017. We can become stronger and we can not allow ourselves to be influenced by the world also through the contribution of the formation, development, maintenance and usage of trustworthy behavior.

2018. We can prevent some failures also through the contribution of the formation, development, maintenance and usage of trustworthy behavior.

2019. Our future can be projected and achieved also through the contribution of the formation, development, maintenance and usage of trustworthy behavior.

2020. Stress can be prevented also through the formation, development, maintenance and usage of trustworthy behavior.

Tolerance

2021. A great capacity of assuming the necessary risks for achieving great successes helps us maintain our tolerance.

2022. A great capacity of remaining involved in the same area with even greater objectives helps us maintain our tolerance.

2023. A great capacity of thinking largely helps us maintain our tolerance.

2024. A great capacity of using available ideas helps us maintain our tolerance.

2025. A great capacity of being flexible helps us maintain our tolerance.

2026. A great capacity of using attitudes helps us maintain our tolerance.

2027. Constructive thinking makes us have zero tolerance towards everybody.

2028. Constructive thinking makes us have zero tolerance towards some people's influence.

2029. Positive thinking makes us have zero tolerance towards negative thinking.

2030. Constructive thinking makes us have zero tolerance towards discrimination.

2031. A low tolerance for personal imperfections contributes a lot to have more chances to meet more favorable situations.

2032. A low tolerance for personal imperfections contributes a lot to having more chances to meet more favorable situations.

2033. A low tolerance for personal imperfections helps us a lot to achieve true friendships.

2034. A low tolerance for personal imperfections helps us a lot to achieve effective co operations.

2035. A low tolerance for personal imperfections helps us a lot to achieve our personal objectives faster.

2036. Low tolerance for personal imperfections contributes a lot in achieving success in life.

Training

2037. A full compatibility of training with the objectives is an engine of progress.

2038. A full compatibility of training with the objectives helps us become even more efficient.

2039. A full compatibility of training with the objectives helps us achieve a beautiful life.

2040. A full compatibility of training with the objectives is achieved also through efficient accomplishments of social reality.

2041. A complete compatibility of training with the objectives assures success in life.

2042. The desire of recognition and training mobilizes people to achieve successes.

2043. A full compatibility of training with objectives helps in achieving outstanding performances.

2044. A complete compatibility of training with the objectives helps us meet more favorable situations.

2045. A complete compatibility of training with objectives helps us achieve a more beautiful life.

2046. Each of us is necessary to have the personal objective of the continuous development and training of positive thinking, every day, for as long as we live.

2047. Full compatibility of training with the objective helps us achieve more and greater successes.

2048. How we live day by day, achieving the target of personal training and development of our creative skills helps and contributes greatly to achieving other personal objectives.

2049. Continuously, every day it is necessary to have as a personal objective the training and development of those qualities that help us and contribute to the achievement of personal goals.

2050. At present, step by step, day by day we can get more information useful to us for the training and development of our wisdom. This makes us forever increase our chances of becoming happy rather than build, forge our own happiness. We have everything we need available to us in order to achieve happiness, it only depends on ourselves if we act effectively and persevering to achieve it.

2051. States need and must ensure the legislation of financial and material resources for the continuous training, development and application of the science of raising children.

Uncontrollable

2052. Those who have high preferences for uncontrollable positive activism have the potential and big chances to achieve great outstanding performances.

2053. Those who have high preferences for uncontrollable positive activism have a high potential of achieving a happy life.

2054. Those who have big preferences for positive uncontrollable activism have potential and great chances to achieve a true mature love.

2055. Those who have big preferences for positive uncontrollable activism contribute a lot to many exchanges of information.

Upset

2056. When one of the spouses is upset by the other's behavior he or she must tell the other spouse.

2057. Let us not think about what makes us upset.

2058. Sometimes some people are upset for what they shouldn't be upset about.

2059. Some people are so stupid that they harm themselves only to upset others.

2060. Unconsidered words upset us.

2061. Even if our mother upsets us and is wrong we have no right to wear a rancor.

2062. When we are upset it is good to do something to get out of this state.

2063. When we are upset it is best to go and rest.

2064. We hurt our marriage if we upset with annoyances those whom we married.

2065. There are many situations in which we are upset, tired, depressed, stressed, etc.. and then, in these situations it is necessary to read as many ideas as possible, collected in books, etc..

Values

2066. Life is much more beautiful in a marriage when they have a shared values system.

2067. The common values of friends make them cooperate.

2068. The common values of friends make them understand each other better.

2069. The common values of friends make them feel better.

2070. The common values of friends increase their confidence in the strength of their friendship.

2071. The common values of friends increase the chances that their friendship last for as long as they live.

2072. Common values make friendships stronger.

2073. Common values are like a common language.

2074. Common values create more security between friends.

2075. The choices we make are taken according to the values we have.

2076. Our own values help us progress more or less.

2077. Moral values continuously increase our credibility.

2078. Moral values help us a lot in maintaining effective co operations.

2079. Spiritual values help us realize a happy marriage.

2080. People who have spiritual values are more likely to achieve their personal goals.

2081. Moral values help us a lot to maintain a happy marriage.

2082. Spiritual values help us a lot to achieve more successes.

2083. People who also have spiritual values can more easily solve the problems they need to resolve.

2084. Moral values make us more credible.

2085. Moral values help us a lot to achieve effective co operations.

2086. Spiritual values help us a lot to maintain our marriage happy.

2087. People who also have spiritual values have increased chances of achieving more friendships.

2088. Moral values create most of the times great masterpieces.

2089. Spiritual values help us achieve more effective co operations.

2090. People who also have spiritual values have greater chances to achieve outstanding performances.

2091. Spiritual values help us a lot to achieve true friendships.

2092. People who also have spiritual values have greater chances to achieve more successes.

2093. People who respect their collaborators have more humanist values.

2094. People with human social behaviors have their own value system of humanist values.

2095. Working in teams of people with similar values helps us achieve efficient global co operations.

2096. People who have spiritual values have more chances to achieve more and greater successes.

Trust-worthy

2097. The trust-worthy man has much more chances to achieve a happy marriage.

2098. Our happiness depends a lot also on the formation, development, maintenance and usage of trustworthy behavior.

2099. Acting efficiently helps us become trustworthy.

2100. A trust-worthy a man has the potential to help him achieve a more beautiful life.

Truth

2101. Hiding the truth can produce many failures.

2102. Ignoring the truth leads to many divorces.

2103. Ignoring the truth is very harmful in the achievement of our happiness.

Unhappy

2104. People who have not succeeded in building a happy marriage up to a certain date need to study deeply the books written about achieving a happy marriage, in order to identify the cause of the lack of achievement or maintenance of an unhappy marriage.

2105. If there were much more happy marriages in the world there would be less unhappy children.

2106. It is certain that if spouses would give the attention and time needed to maintain a happy marriage they would succeed and there would be less unhappy marriages and divorce.

Vigilant

2107. A vigilant man has more chances to become wiser.

2108. A vigilant man has more chances to achieve a happy marriage.

2109. A vigilant man has more chances to achieve a more beautiful life.

Violence

2110. Women are mostly abused in family violence.

2111. Family violence must be prevented through the contribution of all family members.

2112. Family violence stops the achievement of objectives.

Waiting

2113. I have as a personal priority to achieve an increasing number of constructive, effective, harmonious relations, with mutual trust with as many people as possible from all countries to cooperate effectively and support each other in achieving the personal objectives of each of us. Together we acomplish a lot of great deeds. I would be happy for people who read my writings and agree and apply one or more ideas to build as more and more efficient cooperations as they can for each of us and for mankind. The possibilities and potential co operations are endless with me because I have projects in areas which may involve a large number of people. Waiting with confidence and very high expectations for your cooperation with concrete proposals in areas of activity and actions that we want to achieve and any idea, opinion, etc.

Wisdom

2114. Caution and the art of being cautious is a part of wisdom that is good, useful, but necessary and required to continuously develop and apply it always where it is necessary in life.

2115. Abstention is partly, the art of knowing how to abstain within the family, in the relations with the other, with children, other family members (parents, parents-in-law, grandparents, brothers, brothers-in law, etc.), it is a part of the wisdom of each of the spouses, that is useful for us to develop.

2116. At present, step by step, day by day we can get more information useful to us for the training and development of our wisdom. This makes us forever increase our chances of becoming happy rather than build, forge our own happiness. We have everything we need available to us in order to achieve happiness, it only depends on ourselves if we act effectively and persevering to achieve it.

2117. Enormous ammounts of information and a very good quality of many pieces of information from the Internet help us unlimitedly and at an affordable price in the formation and development of our wisdom in an unlimited, virtually free way.

2118. At present, but especially more and more every day we can develop ourselves through cooperation and very much our wisdom primarily by free and unlimited access to the Internet. Each family is vital to have at least one Internet connection or more depending on the number of family members.

2119. Fortunately, in the present and in the future we can continuously and easily develop all the wisdom that we want, provided that we continuously act to develop our wisdom.

2120. Wisdom is a treasure of ours that we can continuously increase as long as we live in an unlimited way which no one can ever take away, but only destroy it in certain situations wholly or partially by degradation in one way or another by: 1) damage, brain illness, 2) the psyche's damage or of a part of the psychological, 3) through some mental illness, 4) through illness with certain diseases that affect, directly or indirectly, wisdom, etc..

2121. Some say that the greatest treasure of all is love. Love is a great treasure, which also makes other treasures greater ones or simply creates treasures. Indeed there are situations, moments in which love for us is the greatest treasure, however we can not generalize that this is the greatest treasure of life automatically. If we can look deeply in a general way we can not practically determine which the greatest treasure is. For example, our wisdom can be evaluated as the largest treasure for many reasons. Usually the wise manage to achieve true love and retain it. Without wisdom is very difficult to make and keep a true love. When wisdom disappears or the wise makes big mistakes that adversely affects love very much, or sometimes even destroys it can be seen what a great treasure wisdom is and how much love depends on wisdom.

2122. The developing of our wisdom is a treasure that we can continuously grow if we continuously act in that sense.

2123. Wisdom is not given to us through birth. We form and develop it along our life.

2124. Tact is part of our wisdom. (Those who have tact will succeed in having more and greater successes.)

2125. Good deeds are a result of wisdom.

2126. Wisdom is a resource to our future wealth.

2127. Wisdom helps us avoid many mistakes.

Will

2128. Will power helps us achieve more favorable chances.

2129. The willpower of not allowing ourselves to be stopped helps us achieve more efficient co operations.

2130. Will power helps us achieve more performances.

2131. The will of going against everyone else's beliefs helps us achieve more pleasant surprises.

2132. The will of going against everyone else's beliefs helps us achieve more favorable situations.

2133. The willpower of not allowing ourselves to be stopped helps us achieve more records.

2134. Will power helps us achieve more records.

2135. The willpower of not allowing ourselves to be stopped helps us achieve more successes.

2136. The will of going against everyone else's beliefs helps us achieve more personal goals.

2137. The willpower of not allowing ourselves to be stopped helps us achieve more favorable situations.

2138. The willpower of not allowing ourselves to be stopped helps us achieve much good luck.

2139. The will of going against everyone else's beliefs helps us achieve more favorable chances.

2140. The more we are, us that work to make as many people as possible happy, the more happiness there will be on this earth.

2141. Ignorance can be prevented if we have will.

2142. Illiteracy should be prevented because of the continuous resources that exist, but there is no will where illiteracy is.

2143. Negative actions can help us at a moment, but they will harm us eventually.

2144. Even if the sly actions can help us at a moment, they will harm us eventually.

2145. The more distant the future is the more the factors that will influence it will be more numerous and some more unknown to us.

2146. Most of us think about the future, our future, the future of our children, the future of our loved ones, the future of our country, the future of the world, of what it will be like in the future and how it will be.

2147. When we work with dedication and confidence in our personal objectives, often we will solve them.

2148. If you know and apply the principles that lead us to successes we will achieve a lot and many successes.

Wishes

2149. Wishes, for the sake of wills can be without any limitation but a realistic criterion. These can vary enormously from person to person as they are.

2150. Our desires are very numerous in some and no less numerous in others. In fact, if we had wishes limted only to the realistic and possible ones to achieve, we will fulfill them if we will act to satisfy them or not.

Wiser

2151. Through cooperation we can become wiser more quickly.

2152. We become wiser through our own reflection and learn from others, from their experience.

2153. Each of us can become wiser freely without offering something in exchange to others every day, if we reflect, every day, on everything that can help us achieve better, faster, all our present and future objectives.

2154. The wiser we are, the more chances we have to meet several favorable occasions.

2155. Wisdom helps us become wiser.

2156. Permanent self education helps us become wiser.

2157. The wiser we are the more chances we have of achieving our personal goals.

2158. The wiser we are the more chances we have to achieve more and greater successes.

2159. The wiser we are the more chances we have of meeting more favorable situations.

2160. The wiser we are the more chances we have to achieve true friendships.

2161. Efficient friendships make some of us wiser.

2162. Communicative women have more chances to become wiser.

2163. A vigilant man has more chances to become wiser.

2164. AGC mediations help us become wiser.

2165. Inter-human communication sometimes helps us become wiser.

2166. Mutual trust helps us become wiser.

2167. Continuously making ourselves efficient helps us become wiser.

Work

2168. Passion for our work helps us achieve more pleasant surprises.

2169. Passion for our work helps us achieve more true friendships.

2170. Life can be more beautiful if we set as a priority the objective of achieving a good life and if we continuously work to achieve this objective.

Worried

2171. Those who have or will have children, love your children, take care of them, always help them when they need your help, even if you are more or less worried. Do not ever forget that you have children.

2172. People who have success are mostly not worried.

2173. Those who have high objectives in life have the necessary qualities to face states of being worried.

Worries

2174. Preventing worries helps us achieve more favorable situations.

2175. Preventing worries helps us achieve more true friendships.

2176. Preventing worries helps us achieve more successes.

2177. If you have had failures you should not worry but continue what you have started if it is positive.

Yourself

2178. In order to change the desire of changing into reality it is necessary to form, develop, maintain and use the ability to have confidence in yourself.

2179. Usually, when you give yourself to the other, you provoke him to give himself to you.

2180. Knowing yourself is very necessary and very useful to us in order to achieve a happy marriage, to maintain it, to make friends and to maintain them, to use cover our qualities and flaws, etc.

Biography

Gheorghe Cornel Ardelean was born on March 11.1954 in place Macea, Arad Country Romania Graduate of Economic University, Craiova Romania

1979-1989 Economist and Chief Economist and sales Department

In 1990-founding member of the first Parliament of Romania after the Revolution of 1989 in PCNU (Provisional Council of National Unity)

1992 - Independent candidate for deputy in the Romanian Parliament, Chamber of Deputies

1992-1996 Advisor to the Arad Country Council as an independent adviser

1992-1996 President of the Commission trade, tourism, services advise Arad Country Council

1990-2002 Director, manager of private companies wholesale

1980 - Philosopher and author books.

1980 He published 118 books, articles in publications, of which 50 English books and 68 books in Romanian

In 2009 - Member and Coordinator of Department programs, projects and activities of the non-profit. International Organisation Cornel Gheorghe Ardelean (OIAGC)

As a thought on long-term, positive, constructive, open, creative, humanistic, etc. It has a great ability to create so many positive ideas and solutions, constructive, humanist, creative, helpful people to achieve what they want. Thinking and ideas sustain and promote the rights of children, women, all people in the world, positive thinking and ideas, constructive, humanistic, tolerante, progressive, understanding and peace between peoples and nations.